The XXL Keto Air Fryer Cookbook for UK

365-Day of Easy and Quick Low Carb Recipes with Tips and Tricks for Keto Dieters to Air Fry Everyday

Sara S. Nelson

Copyright© 2022 By Sara S. Nelson

All Rights Reserved

This book is copyright protected. It is only for personal use. You cannot amend, distribute, sell, use, quote or paraphrase any part of the content within this book, without the consent of the author or publisher.

Under no circumstances will any blame or legal responsibility be held against the publisher, or author, for any damages, reparation, or monetary loss due to the information contained within this book, either directly or indirectly.

Disclaimer Notice:

Please note the information contained within this document is for educational and entertainment purposes only. All effort has been executed to present accurate, up to date, reliable, complete information. No warranties of any kind are declared or implied. Readers acknowledge that the author is not engaged in the rendering of legal, financial, medical or professional advice. The content within this book has been derived from various sources. Please consult a licensed professional before attempting any techniques outlined in this book.

By reading this document, the reader agrees that under no circumstances is the author responsible for any losses, direct or indirect, that are incurred as a result of the use of the information contained within this document, including, but not limited to, errors, omissions, or inaccuracies.

Table of Content

Introduction — 1

Chapter 1 The Keto Diet 101 — 2

What is Ketogenic Diet? 2
How Does Ketogenic Diet Work? 2
Keto Macros 3
Keto Foods to Eat and Avoid 5
Steps to Keto Success 6
Guidelines for Setting a Keto Meal Plan 7

Chapter 2 Air Fryer for Keto — 8

Why Air Fryer for Keto? 8
Air Fryer Cooking Tips 9
Air Fryer Pantry List for Keto 10
Air Fryer Accessory 12

Chapter 3 Breakfast — 13

Blueberry Muffin 14
Broccoli and Mushroom Frittata 14
Bacon Lettuce Wraps 14
Ham with Avocado 14
Gold Muffin 15
Simple Ham and Pepper Omelet 15
Sausage Egg Cup 15
Lemony Cake 15
Pecan and Almond Granola 16
Cauliflower with Avocado 16
Golden Biscuits 16
Cauliflower Hash Browns 18
Sausage with Peppers 18
Broccoli Frittata 18
Egg with Cheddar 18
Spinach Omelet 19
Chocolate Chip Muffin 19
Ham Egg 19
Spinach and Tomato Egg 20
Pepperoni Egg 20

Chapter 4 Vegetable and Meatless — 21

Super Cheese Cauliflower Fritters 22
Cheese-Broccoli Fritters 22
Aubergine Lasagna 22
Cheddar Green Beans 23
Tofu with Chili-Galirc Sauce 23
Asparagus with Broccoli 23
Courgette and Mushroom Kebab 23
Broccoli Croquettes 24
Spinach Cheese Casserole 24
Cheese Stuffed Pepper 24
Aubergine with Tomato and Cheese 24
Courgette with Spinach 26
Cauliflower with Cheese 26
Riced Cauliflower with Eggs 26

Mushroom Soufflés 26	Mushroom with Artichoke and Spinach 27
Roast Aubergine and Courgette Bites 27	Broccoli with Herbed Garlic Sauce 28
Citrus Courgette Balls 27	Cheese Stuffed Courgette 28

Chapter 5 Meat and Poultry — 29

Ham Chicken with Cheese 30	Buttery Strip Steak 33
Lime Marinated Lamb Chop 30	Courgette Noodle with Beef Meatball 33
Skirt Steak Carne Asada 30	Lush Spiced Ribeye Steak 35
Pork Tenderloin with Ricotta 31	Chicken Breast with Coriander and Lime 35
Pork Cutlets with Red Wine 31	Roasted Chicken Leg with Leeks 35
Herbed Lamb Chops with Parmesan 31	Loin Steak with Mayo 35
Crispy Pork Chop with Parmesan 32	Aromatic Pork Loin Roast 36
Beef Chuck with Brussels Sprouts 32	Bacon-Wrapped Cheese Pork 36
Spicy Chicken Roll-Up with Monterey Jack 32	Pork Meatballs 37
Turkey Sausage with Cauliflower 33	Skirt Steak with Rice Vinegar 37

Chapter 6 Fish and Seafood — 38

Savory Prawns 39	Mackerel with Spinach 41
Swordfish Skewers with Cherry Tomato 39	Prawn with Swiss Chard 41
Prawns with Romaine 39	Tilapia with Balsamic Vinegar 43
Grilled Tuna Cake 40	Salmon Fritters with Courgette 43
Lemony Salmon Steak 40	Lemony Salmon 43
Tuna Avocado Bites 40	Salmon with Cauliflower 43
Whitefish Fillet with Green Bean 40	Golden Prawn 43
Tuna Steak 41	Rosemary Prawn Skewers 44
Sweet Tilapia Fillets 41	Basil Salmon Fillet 44
Roast Swordfish Steak 41	Snapper with Shallot and Tomato 44

Chapter 7 Snack and Dessert — 45

Strawberry Pecan Pie 46	Spinach Chips 48
Chocolate Chips Soufflés 46	Kale Chips 48
Chocolate Brownies 46	Salami Roll-Ups 48
Whiskey Chocolate Brownies 47	Orange Custard 48
Calamari Rings 47	Pepperoni Chips 50
Avocado Fries 47	Bacon-Wrapped Onion Rings 50

Coconut Tart with Walnuts 50	Berry Compote with Coconut Chips 51
Air Fried Aubergine 50	Courgette Fries 51
Mixed Berry Pots 50	Coconut and Chocolate Pudding 52
Provolone Cheese Balls 51	Chicken Nuggets 52

Appendix 1: Measurement Conversion Chart — 53

Appendix 2: 365-Day Meal Plan — 54

Appendix 3: Air Fryer Time Table — 61

Appendix 4: Dirty Dozen and Clean Fifteen — 63

Appendix 5: Recipes Index — 64

Introduction

If you've already used an air fryer prior, you'll probably know that it is a revolutionary cooking apparatus that can make you live better and save your time. But even so, what is special about this piece of the appliance?

Air fryers have what it takes to replace microwave, oven dehydrator, deep fryer while preparing some of the most delicious meals you've ever tasted in a shorter time. If you have a very busy schedule and you still plan to cook some healthy meals for your family, then air fryers are your best bet.

They can also be useful with our overall commitment and success to the ketogenic diet scheme. Long-term triumph on the keto diet scheme is attributable to how you easily prepare your meals. And that is why we recommend air fryers for your ketogenic diet journey to help you prepare your meals, especially on days when you are very busy and need all the time in the world.

Throughout this cookbook, you'll learn all you need to know about some ketogenic diet air fryer recipes, why you should use air fryers in the preparation of your diets, and some of the basics of being successful with the keto diet scheme. Let's cook!

Chapter 1 The Keto Diet 101

What is Ketogenic Diet?

Practically all known diets, to varying degrees, concentrate on either lowering the levels of calories or just manipulating the rate of the intake of one of the three important macronutrients (proteins, fats, or carbohydrates) to get the same results.

Ketogenic diets are a group of special diets that have a very high concentration of fats but with a very low carbohydrate concentration. The term "ketogenic" typically means the increased production of ketone bodies caused by the high rate of lipolysis (the breakdown of fats). Ketones are acid byproducts formed during the intermediate breakdown of "fat" into "fatty acids" by the liver.

Today, ketogenic diet advocates firmly believe that carbohydrates, especially those with a high glycemic index, are some of the major factors why several people add weight.

Carbohydrate foods are usually digested to produce glucose, a simple form of sugar that is generally considered the body's preferred energy source because it is fast-burning energy that is readily available after a meal.

Even though the human body can digest glycogen and fats to produce energy for its use, it prefers to get it from carbohydrates because it is an easy route.

Ketogenic diets are designed to "force" the body to use up its endogenous glucose stores and then make it switch to the fat stores as the main energy-generating equivalent for the body.

Although the ketogenic diet is known for its rapid weight loss advantage, especially in the early stages of the diet practice, weight loss is surely a moderate and tedious process.

How Does Ketogenic Diet Work?

To know how the ketogenic diet works, it is important to know the physiology behind it. The type of change that the body undergoes when it is undergoing ketogenesis is known as ketosis. The term "Ketosis" often causes skepticism or even fear in those who try as much as possible to decide if it is a good thing. Below is an easy insight into what ketosis means.

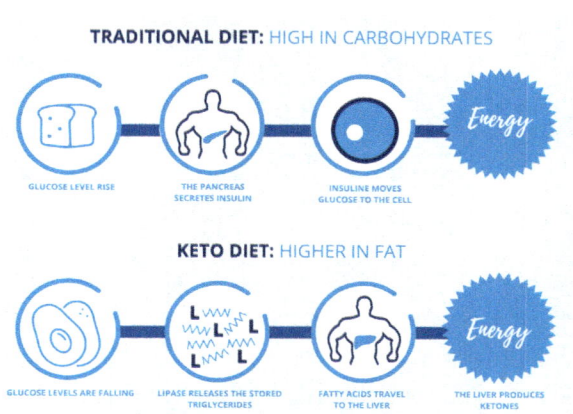

Ketosis simply denotes that the body has stopped using carbohydrates as its source of fuel and then switches to fat almost exclusively as its alternative energy source.

But then it can get a little more complex than that. Ketosis starts when there are low levels of carbohydrates (specifically, glucose) in the blood to replenish the endogenous glycogen stores in the liver.

What then is this glycogen? Glycogen can simply be seen as long and branched chains of glucose molecules joined end-to-end in a certain manner to confer the right chemical integrity to it. The liver produces glycogen from carbohydrates as a fast-food source for the body after a carbohydrate-rich meal.

A lack of carbohydrates means that the body needs an alternative food source to compensate for the enormous amount of energy required in its daily processes. So then the body makes use of its fat stores, especially fatty acids.

The liver breaks down these fats into compounds which are ultimately converted to ketone bodies through series of chemical reactions that are highly specialized for that process.

When the liver then discharges these ketone bodies into the bloodstream to utilize as energy, this is ketosis in its simplest definition.

When you eat carbohydrates rich foods, your body uses them for energy generation and converts the undigested ones into fat making use of insulin.

What this means is that carbohydrates are not stored in your body, except those stored in your liver as glycogen molecules.

If you do not replenish the carbohydrates in your blood after using them, your body will eventually use the fats you consume with your food and the fats stored in the body as fuel. Ketosis usually begins at about 48 hours after the last carbohydrate meal.

Keto Macros

The most common macros nutrient ratio for keto diets is 25% protein, 5% carbohydrates, and 70% fats. In certain cases, some nutritionists and dieticians will recommend that you increase the fat percentage to about 75% and decrease that of protein to about 20%.

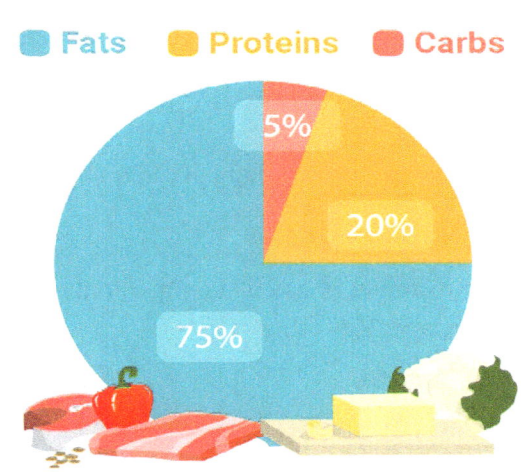

Also, you can check another substitute for the average keto diet: the cyclic ketogenic diet. This type of diet is advised for individuals who are trying to decrease their fat mass and increase their muscle mass. While observing this diet, you will have to control your food intake to the standard ketogenic diet for about five to six days, and then one to two days of raised carbohydrates consumption. What this diet attempts to do is to restore your blood glucose level.

Steps to Getting your Macro Right

1. Determine your exact calorie need (Cal/day)

Here's how to calculate it for men and women.

- Men

10 x weight (kilogram) + 6.25 x height (cm) - 5 x age (y) + 5

- Women

10 x weight (kilogram) + 6.25 x height (cm) - 5 x age (y) - 161

Then multiply your result by an activity factor.

- Resting: x 1.2
- Slightly active: x 1,375
- Moderately active: x 1.55
- Very active: x 1.725
- Extra active: x 1.9

The result gives you your total daily energy expenditure.

2. Decide on the ideal distribution of your macronutrients

Typical macronutrient recommendations are as follows:

- Carbohydrates: 45 to 65% of total calories
- Fat: 20 to 35% of total calories
- Protein: 10 to 35% of the total number of calories

A person who follows a ketogenic diet would need a lot more fat and fewer carbohydrates, while an endurance athlete might need a higher carbohydrate intake.

3. Follow your macros and your caloric intake

There are many user-friendly tools specifically designed to simplify tracking macros.

Many applications have a barcode reader that automatically enters a portion of a scanned food into your macro log.

You can also write macros manually in a physical log. The method depends on your individual preferences.

4. Counting example

Here is an example of calculating macronutrients for a 2000 calorie diet consisting of 40% carbohydrate, 30% protein, and 30% fat.

* *Carbohydrates:*

- 4 calories per gram
- 40% of 2,000 calories = 800 calories of carbohydrate per day
- Total grams of carbohydrate allowed per day = 800/4 = 200 grams

* *Protein:*

- 4 calories per gram
- 30% of 2,000 Cal = 600 Cal of protein per day
- Total protein allowed gram/day = 600/4 = 150 grams

* *Fats:*
  - 9 calories per gram
  - 30% of 2,000 Cal = 600 Cal of protein/day
  - Total fat allowed (gram/day) = 600/9 = 67 grams

Keto Foods to Eat and Avoid

Keto-Friendly Foods to Eat

When you are sticking to the ketogenic diet scheme, there are some foods should constitute your diet and some that you should avoid.

Examples of keto-centric foods are:

- **Eggs:** Organic and pastured eggs.
- **Poultry:** Turkey and chicken.
- **Fatty fish:** Mackerel, herring, and wild-caught salmon.
- **Meat:** Pork, venison, grass-fed beef, bison, and organ meats.
- **Full-fat dairy:** Cream, butter, and yogurt.
- **Full-fat cheese:** Brie, mozzarella, cheddar, cream cheese, and goat cheese.
- **Seeds and nuts:** Almonds, macadamia nuts, pumpkin seeds, walnuts, flaxseeds, and peanuts.

- **Nut butter:** Cashew butter, almond, and natural peanut.
- **Healthy fats:** Avocado oil, olive oil, coconut oil, sesame oil, and coconut butter.
- **Avocados:** You can add whole avocados to almost any snack or meal.
- **Non-starchy vegetables:** Tomatoes, broccoli, greens, peppers, and mushrooms.
- **Condiments:** Vinegar, pepper, salt, spices, fresh herbs, and lemon juice.

Foods to Stay Away From

When you are observing the ketogenic diet, there are some foods that you need to stay away from. These are generally foods that are rich in carbohydrates. Below are some of the foods that you should avoid to get the most in your ketogenic diet commitments.

- **Baked Foods and Bread:** Whole-wheat bread, white bread, cookies, crackers, rolls, and doughnuts.
- **Sugary and Sweets Foods:** Ice cream, sugar, maple syrup, candy, coconut sugar, and agave syrup.
- **Sweetened Beverages:** Juice, soda, sports drinks, and sweetened teas.
- **Pasta:** Noodles and spaghetti.
- **Grain products and Grains:** Rice, wheat, tortillas, breakfast cereals, and oats.
- **Starchy vegetables:** Sweet potatoes, potatoes, corn, butternut squash, pumpkin, and peas.
- **Legumes and Beans:** Chickpeas, black beans, kidney beans, and lentils.
- **Fruit:** Grapes, citrus, pineapples, and bananas.
- **High-carb Sauces:** Dipping sauces, sugar-rich salad dressings, and Barbecue sauce.
- **Some Alcoholic Beverages:** Sugar-rich mixed beverages and beer.

Even though it is not advisable to consume carbohydrate-rich foods when you are on the ketogenic diet scheme, fruits with low-glycemic values like berries may be taken in restricted amounts if you are sticking to a keto-centric macronutrient range.

Steps to Keto Success

1. Know the Right Amount of Macronutrients You Need

Knowing the exact amount of fat, carbs, and protein that you need during a ketogenic diet exercise is the most important step that you need to take when drafting the perfect ketogenic diet menu.

2. Understand Your Exact Macro Requirements

You also need the precise macro requirements that will help you enter the state of ketosis and help you regulate your energy levels as it supports your body fitness objectives. Like we discussed earlier, a macro calculator will help you approximate your nutritional portion. For example, to calculate the percentage of your macros, divide the calorie values by the value of the micronutrients you consume daily and multiply by 100%.

Example of Keto Macros Calculation:

- Your carbs requirement is (80g/1800g) x 100% = 5%

- Your protein requirement (600g/1800g) x 100% = 33%
- Your fats requirement (1,120g/1800g) x 100% = 62%

Hence, the total amount of calories should sum up to 100% (5% + 33 %+ 62% = 100).

3. Pick the Best Keto-Centric Foods

When you've ascertained your macro objectives, then get busy selecting some of the best ketogenic-centric foods that match your macros.

4. Know Your Servings

When you completely come to terms with the number of carbs, fat, and protein that you need to consume, then the next thing to do is to know the serving amount that is right for you. Becoming a master in this can take a bit of practice and time, but one good way to learning this is to carefully track the food amount that you eat every day.

Guidelines for Setting a Keto Meal Plan

As noted before, certain individuals need to decrease the levels of their carbs intake if they must enter the state of ketosis.

Adapting to a ketogenic diet scheme can sometimes be overpowering, but it does not have to be hard.

You should concentrate on decreasing your carbohydrate consumption while raising the levels of your protein and fat intake of your snacks and meals. You must limit your intake of carb if you must enter a state of ketosis.

While it is true that some people can enter the ketosis state by just consuming twenty grams of carbohydrates a day, some others may need higher to achieve the same feat.

The general rule is that you'll achieve ketosis faster if you lower your carbs intake. Thus, committing to eating carbs-rich foods would make you lose weight faster if you are practicing the ketogenic regimen.

A healthy keto diet should comprise about 10-30% protein, 75% fat, and no greater than 20 to 50 grams or 5%of carbohydrates per day.

Focus on low-carb, high-fat foods like meats, eggs, low-carb vegetables, and dairy, in addition to sugar-free beverages. Ensure that you limit your consumption of unhealthy fats and highly processed foods.

Even though a lot of keto-based foods are centered on animal products, the scheme has a lot of vegetarian alternatives that you can settle for too.

If you are sticking to a more accommodating ketogenic diet scheme, including small carbohydrate veggies in your dinner or one cup of berries for breakfast will raise the number of carbohydrates in your ketogenic meal plan.

Chapter 2 Air Fryer for Keto

Air fryers are a very helpful and popular cooking appliance that you can use to prepare different air fryer-based ketogenic recipes. And with their fantastic cooking ability, air fryers can also make your dishes more tasteful.

Also, the process of air frying is super easy, quick, and convenient. It is important to note that the process does not supernaturally make carbohydrates vanish. It can only provide different recipe types that are low carbohydrates and keto.

With an air fryer, you can reduce the amount of oil that you use in the preparation of the recipes and make cooking time shorter. This implies that you can browse recipes that are keto-friendly and low in carbohydrate content.

Keto air fryer recipes include meals consumed at different times, such as dinner, lunch, breakfast, and some other indulgent keto desserts.

Why Air Fryer for Keto?

- **Prepare Keto-Based Diets with Minimal Efforts**

With an air fryer, you can prepare certain kinds of ketogenic diets in less than an hour. Some of these recipes even take a much lower time to prepare.

- **Prepare Nice Hard-Boiled Eggs with Ease**

It is indeed a fun fact to know that you don't need to hard-boiled for preparing hard-boiled eggs with air fryers. Just position the eggs inside the air fryer space and have the timer set for 260°F and sixteen minutes.

- **Prepare Keto Breaded Crispy Snacks**

Air fryers are helpful to those who prepare keto breaded crispy snacks. For example, you can prepare super simple air-fried crunchy pickles with an air fryer by making beading from crushed pork rinds and grated Parmesan cheese.

- **Quick Keto Snacks**

One satisfying and easy idea for quick keto snacks is to prepare wrapped salami mozzarella cheese sticks with air fryers.

Slice the cheese sticks to one-third of its size. Coat each of them with a salami piece and keep them in place using a toothpick. Put it inside an air fryer and allow it to cook at 360°F Fahrenheit for six minutes.

- **Make Meats Juicy and Delicious**

The application of air fryers for use in cooking keto-based meals is far beyond snacks and fries.

You can prepare wonderful burgers with this powerful kitchen appliance. Also, you can cook mid-sized patties at 350° for about ten minutes, or just when they've reached the preferred doneness.

- **Prepare Fantastic Keto Fries for Your Burger**

You probably do not know that jicama is an amazing substitute for potatoes in preparing keto French fries? You can toss these jicama fries inside your air fryer and set the temperature to 400°F and cook for twenty minutes. The experience is worthy of your trial.

- **Make Keto-Centric Vegetable Crisps**

With air fryers, you can easily prepare Brussels sprouts that will be tender inside and crispy outside without cooking for eternity. Ten minutes is sufficient to prepare for this amazing and tasteful meal.

- **Prepare Mess-Free Bacon**

The duration of cooking will differ contingently on how thick the bacon is, but you can prepare crispy, traditional bacon at 390°F in just eight minutes. If the bacon is thick, then the duration of cooling can last up to eleven minutes or more if you want your bacon to be very crispy.

Some other reasons why an air fryer is a great option for you!

- Unlike other difficult cooking options, the ease of using of air fryers is one of its strong points.
- Cleaning this kitchen apparatus is very easy. Plus air fryers are portable so that you can convey them to different places without breaking a sweat.
- You can conveniently remove the air fryer's basket to see if food is done cooking and then just place it back in to cook longer if desired.
- As noted earlier, the duration of cooking is faster when the device is an air fryer. It cooks faster than most traditional ovens out there!
- Cook time is also the literal meaning and you don't have to waste extra time preheating the cooking apparatus or waiting for the device to attain the desired pressure, as in the case of pressure cookers.
- The temperature of the kitchen will be cooler if you are using an air fryer. This is unlike the case of conventional ovens which heighten your kitchen's temperature.

Air Fryer Cooking Tips

Have Your Air Fryer Preheated

If you bring an air fryer that does not come with preheat settings, then set it to your preferred temperature and let it work for some three minutes before putting your food inside.

Utilize Oil on Certain Foods

There are some types of foods that you can make crisp using oil. Some others do not require oil to achieve the same results.

Lubricate the Air Fryer Basket

Take a little time and lubricate the basket of your air fryer. Get this done even the food you are preparing does not need oil. This helps prevent the food from becoming non-sticky.

* Use Aerosol Spray Cans

Using an aerosol spray can can keep food from sticking on the air fryer basket, and thus reduce the burden of cleaning it.

* Do Not Choke the Air Fryer Basket

If you desire that your fried meals become crispy, then you must keep the basket relatively free. Don't stuff it with too many things. If you do, you risk preventing whatever you are preparing from browning and crisping. If you don't want this to occur, then prepare your meal in different batches or buy a larger air fryer.

* Shake the Basket

When you are preparing smaller food like French fries, chicken wings, it makes sense that you frequently shake the air fryer basket for some minutes to make sure the cooking is even.

* Spray Midway While Cooking

Foods that are coated need to be sprayed. And, don't forget to spray dry flour patches that will occur midway while air frying your foods.

* Put Water at the Bottom

If you are preparing a greasy meal with your air fryer, do not be astonished if you discover that some white smoke is coming out of the apparatus. All you need to do to address this is to put a small amount of water at the bottom of your device's basket.

* Be Cautious of Petite-Sized Items

All air fryers feature a very effective fan fixed atop them. This fan makes some items with lighter weight to be swept up by the fan and this can be very dangerous.

* Regulate the Temperature for Particular Foods

Sometimes, it can be appealing to crank the temperature of your air fryer to its maximum so that it can work faster, but you need to take great care because certain foods can quickly dry out.

One great rule that works the magic is to regulate the time and heat to the time required for the preparation of the meal you are preparing. If you regulate the temperature below 350°F for twenty minutes in your oven, but for your air fryer, you can decrease the temperature to about 320°F and cook the meal for sixteen minutes.

* Buy a Good Thermometer

You must acquire a quick-read thermometer for your air fryer particularly in the preparation of certain kinds of meats, such as pork, chicken, and steak.

Air Fryer Pantry List for Keto

And so it is time to go for another round of crazy shopping, but you are wondering what you need to settle after you've decided to stick to the ketogenic regimen.

It may seem like rocket science to some, especially when they think about the different keto-based ingredients that they need to buy, but with a few instructions, they can know what is exactly needed.

While some of the inclusions of this list can easily be gotten from shops in the neighborhood, some others may need dedicated search and online ordering if you must use them.

It would be great if you can visit any grocery store around you to know what appeared air-fryer-worthy. Don't limit yourself to the normal suspects and try some unanticipated grocery stuff.

When you do, you will almost always notice that the results will be by-and-large a resounding, fun-filled, and sometimes astonishing success.

Just as you would expect, different products have different duration, and you may need some patience and a handful of trials to do it the right way. Air fryers are somewhat forgiving, so that you may not likely save a severe situation if you did not do the right thing. If needed, deliberately make mistakes on the part of less time than more time until you arrive at your meal choice.

Before then, you need to know what you need for your keto air fryer pantry list. If you go shopping, you should buy the following items:

- **Portable Protein Sources**
  * Canned tuna
  * Canned salmon
  * Hard-boiled eggs
  * Pepperoni
  * Beef meat sticks
  * Cheese
  * Salami
  * Pork rinds
  * Canned sardines
  * Smoked oysters
  * Jerky

- **Healthy Keto Fat Sources**
  * Coconut oil
  * Avocado oil
  * Extra Virgin Olive Oil
  * Grass-fed butter ghee

- **Keto Snacks**
  * Pecans
  * Pili nuts
  * Pumpkin seeds
  * Almonds
  * Unsweetened peanut butter
  * Avocado
  * Walnuts
  * Nutzo
  * Cheese crisps
  * Macadamia nuts
  * Unsweetened almond butter
  * Lily's chocolate bars
  * Unsweetened coconut butter
  * Sunflower seeds
  * Olives single servings

- **Keto Baking Essentials**
  * Coconut unsweetened, shredded
  * Coconut flour
  * Sesame flour
  * Ground flaxseed
  * Unsweetened cocoa powder
  * Almond flour
  * Chia seeds
  * Pork rind breadcrumbs
  * Cacao butter

Chapter 2 Air Fryer for Keto   11

- Baking powder
- Pink Himalayan sea salt
- Bone broth
- Baking soda
- Gelatin
- Cream of tartar
- Apple extract
- Xanthan gum
- Caramel extract
- Almond extract
- Maple extract
- Lemon extract
- Vanilla stevia
- Vanilla extract
- Clear stevia
- Swerve confectioners
- Swerve granular
- Swerve brown sugar
- Sugar-Free chocolate chips
- Monk fruit sweetener
- Whey protein powder
- 85% dark chocolate
- Egg white protein powder

- **Other Pantry Condiments**

- No Sugar Added Ketchup
- Dressings
- Mustard
- Mayo
- No Sugar added tomato sauce
- Lakanto maple syrup

Air Fryer Accessory

There are many quick keto-based air fryer foods to prepare with the assistance of some good air fryer accessories. You can fully indulge in many of these foods that you never imagined could be air-fried. Take your cooking to the next level. But before then, get busy buying some of these air fryer accessories.

- Silicone Trivet
- Tortilla Stand for Crispy Tacos
- Cupcake Cups or Silicon Muffin
- Silicone Tongs
- Deep Baking Pans: Cake Pans or Barrel Pans
- Skewers and Rack
- Silicone Pots
- Shallow Baking Pans or "Pizza Pan"
- Larger Size Air Fryer
- Parchment Sheets

Chapter 3 Breakfast

Blueberry Muffin

Prep time: 5 minutes | Cook time: 15 minutes | Makes 6 muffins

115 g blanched finely ground almond flour
10 g granulated sweetener
4 tbsps. salted butter, melted
2 large eggs, whisked
2 tsps. baking powder
45 g fresh blueberries, chopped

1. In a large bowl, combine all ingredients. Evenly pour batter into six silicone muffin cups greased with cooking spray.
2. Place muffin cups into air fryer basket. Adjust the temperature to 160ºC and set the timer for 15 minutes. Muffins should be golden brown when done.
3. Let the muffins cool in cups 15 minutes to avoid crumbling. Serve warm.

Nutrition Info per Serving:
calories: 269 | fat: 24g | protein: 8g | carbs: 23g | net carbs: 20g | sugar: 12g | fibre: 3g

Bacon Lettuce Wraps

Prep time: 20 minutes | Cook time: 13 minutes | Serves 4

230 g (about 12 slices) reduced-sodium bacon
8 tbsps. mayonnaise
8 large romaine lettuce leaves
4 Roma tomatoes, sliced
Salt and freshly ground black pepper

1. Arrange the bacon in a single layer in the air fryer basket. (It's OK if the bacon sits a bit on the sides.) Set the air fryer to 180ºC and cook for 10 minutes. Check for crispiness and cook for 2 to 3 minutes longer if needed. Cook in batches, if necessary, and drain the grease in between batches.
2. Spread 1 tbsp. of mayonnaise on each of the lettuce leaves and top with the tomatoes and cooked bacon. Season to taste with salt and freshly ground black pepper. Roll the lettuce leaves as you would a burrito, securing with a toothpick if desired.

Nutrition Info per Serving:
calories: 370 | fat: 34g | protein: 11g | carbs: 7g | net carbs: 4g | sugar: 2g | fibre: 3g

Broccoli and Mushroom Frittata

Prep time: 15 minutes | Cook time: 20 minutes | Serves 2

1 tbsp. olive oil
135 g broccoli florets, finely chopped
35 g sliced brown mushrooms
15 g finely chopped onion
½ tsp. salt
¼ tsp. freshly ground black pepper
6 eggs
25 g Parmesan cheese

1. In an 16-cm nonstick cake pan, combine the olive oil, broccoli, mushrooms, onion, salt, and pepper. Stir until the vegetables are thoroughly coated with oil. Place the cake pan in the air fryer basket and set the air fryer to 205°C. Air fry for 5 minutes until the vegetables soften.
2. Meanwhile, in a medium bowl, whisk the eggs and Parmesan until thoroughly combined. Pour the egg mixture into the pan and shake gently to distribute the vegetables. Air fry for another 15 minutes until the eggs are set.
3. Remove from the air fryer and let them sit for 5 minutes to cool slightly. Use a silicone spatula to gently lift the frittata onto a plate before serving.

Nutrition Info per Serving:
calories: 360 | fat: 25g | protein: 25g | carbs: 10g | net carbs: 8g | sugar: 3.4g | fibre: 2g

Ham with Avocado

Prep time: 5 minutes | Cook time: 10 minutes | Serves 2

1 large Hass avocado, halved and pitted
2 thin slices ham
2 large eggs
2 tbsps. chopped spring onions, plus more for garnish
½ tsp. fine sea salt
¼ tsp. ground black pepper
25 g shredded Cheddar cheese (omit for dairy-free)

1. Preheat the air fryer to 205ºC.
2. Place a slice of ham into the cavity of each avocado half. Crack an egg on top of the ham, then sprinkle on the spring onions, salt, and pepper.
3. Place the avocado halves in the air fryer cut side up and cook for 10 minutes, or until the egg is cooked to your desired doneness. Top with the cheese (if using) and cook for 30 seconds or more, or until the cheese is melted. Garnish with chopped spring onions.
4. Best served fresh. Store extras in an airtight container in the fridge for up to 4 days. Reheat in a preheated 180ºC air fryer for a few minutes, until warmed through.

Nutrition Info per Serving:
calories: 307 | fat: 24g | protein: 14g | carbs: 10g | net carbs: 3g | sugar: 4.8g | fibre: 7g

Gold Muffin

Prep time: 5 minutes | Cook time: 15 minutes | Makes 6 muffins

95 g blanched finely ground almond flour
5 g granulated sweetener
2 tbsps. salted butter, melted
1 large egg, whisked
2 tsps. baking powder
1 tsp. ground allspice

1. In a large bowl, combine all ingredients. Evenly pour batter into six silicone muffin cups greased with cooking spray.
2. Place muffin cups into air fryer basket. Adjust the temperature to 160ºC and set the timer for 15 minutes. Cooked muffins should be golden brown.
3. Let the muffins cool in cups 15 minutes to avoid crumbling. Serve warm.

Nutrition Info per Serving:

calories: 160 | fat: 14g | protein: 5g | carbs: 20g | net carbs: 18g | sugar: 6.3g | fibre: 2g

Simple Ham and Pepper Omelet

Prep time: 5 minutes | Cook time: 8 minutes | Serves 1

2 large eggs
60 ml unsweetened, unflavoured almond milk
¼ tsp. fine sea salt
⅛ tsp. ground black pepper
35 g diced ham (omit for vegetarian)
30 g diced green and red peppers
2 tbsps. diced spring onions, plus more for garnish
30 g shredded Cheddar cheese (omit for dairy-free)
Quartered cherry tomatoes, for serving (optional)

1. Preheat the air fryer to 180ºC. Grease a 12 by 6 cm cake pan and set aside.
2. In a small bowl, use a fork to whisk together the eggs, almond milk, salt, and pepper. Add the ham, peppers, and spring onions. Pour the mixture into the greased pan. Add the cheese on top (if using).
3. Place the pan in the basket of the air fryer. Cook for 8 minutes, or until the eggs are cooked to your liking.
4. Loosen the omelet from the sides of the pan with a spatula and place it on a serving plate. Garnish with spring onions and serve with cherry tomatoes, if desired. Best served fresh.

Nutrition Info per Serving:

calories: 476 | fat: 32g | protein: 41g | carbs: 3g | net carbs: 2g | sugar: 14g | fibre: 1g

Sausage Egg Cup

Prep time: 10 minutes | Cook time: 15 minutes | Serves 6

340 g pork sausage meat
6 large eggs
½ tsp. salt
¼ tsp. ground black pepper
½ tsp. crushed red pepper flakes

1. Place sausage in six 8-cm ramekins (about 60 g per ramekin) greased with cooking oil. Press sausage down to cover bottom and about 1-cm up the sides of ramekins. Crack one egg into each ramekin and sprinkle evenly with salt, black pepper, and red pepper flakes.
2. Place ramekins into air fryer basket. Adjust the temperature to 180ºC and set the timer for 15 minutes. Egg cups will be done when sausage is fully cooked to at least 65ºC and the egg is firm. Serve warm.

Nutrition Info per Serving:

calories: 267 | fat: 21g | protein: 14g | carbs: 1g | net carbs: 1g | sugar: 0.2g | fibre: 0g

Lemony Cake

Prep time: 10 minutes | Cook time: 14 minutes | Serves 6

95 g blanched finely ground almond flour
10 g powdered sweetener
½ tsp. baking powder
55 g unsalted butter, melted
60 ml unsweetened almond milk
2 large eggs
1 tsp. vanilla extract
1 medium lemon
1 tsp. poppy seeds

1. In a large bowl, mix almond flour, sweetener, baking powder, butter, almond milk, eggs, and vanilla.
2. Slice the lemon in half and squeeze the juice into a small bowl, then add to the batter.
3. Using a fine grater, zest the lemon and add 1 tbsp. of zest to the batter and stir. Add poppy seeds to batter.
4. Pour batter into nonstick 12-cm round cake pan. Place pan into the air fryer basket.
5. Adjust the temperature to 150ºC and set the timer for 14 minutes.
6. When fully cooked, a toothpick inserted in centre will come out mostly clean. The cake will finish cooking and firm up as it cools. Serve at room temperature.

Nutrition Info per Serving:

calories: 204 | fat: 18g | protein: 6g | carbs: 17g | net carbs: 15g | sugar: 8g | fibre: 2g

Pecan and Almond Granola

Prep time: 10 minutes | Cook time: 5 minutes | Serves 6

220 g pecans, chopped
90 g unsweetened coconut flakes
140 g almond slivers
45 g sunflower seeds
40 g golden flaxseed
40 g low-carb, sugar-free chocolate chips
5 g granulated sweetener
2 tbsps. unsalted butter
1 tsp. ground cinnamon

1. In a large bowl, mix all ingredients.
2. Place the mixture into a round baking dish. Place dish into the air fryer basket.
3. Adjust the temperature to 160ºC and set the timer for 5 minutes.
4. Allow it to cool completely before serving.

Nutrition Info per Serving:
calories: 617 | fat: 55g | protein: 11g | carbs: 32g | net carbs: 21g | sugar: 10.2g | fibre: 11g

Cauliflower with Avocado

Prep time: 15 minutes | Cook time: 8 minutes | Serves 2

1 (340-g) steamer bag cauliflower
1 large egg
45 g shredded Mozzarella cheese
1 ripe medium avocado
½ tsp. garlic powder
¼ tsp. ground black pepper

1. Cook cauliflower according to package instructions. Remove from bag and place into cheesecloth or clean towel to remove excess moisture.
2. Place cauliflower into a large bowl and mix the egg and Mozzarella. Cut a piece of parchment to fit your air fryer basket. Separate the cauliflower mixture into two, and place it on the parchment in two mounds. Press out the cauliflower mounds into a 1/2-cm-thick rectangle. Place the parchment into the air fryer basket.
3. Adjust the temperature to 205ºC and set the timer for 8 minutes.
4. Flip the cauliflower halfway through the cooking time.
5. When the timer beeps, remove the parchment and allow the cauliflower to cool for 5 minutes.
6. Cut open the avocado and remove the pit. Scoop out the inside, place it in a medium bowl, and mash it with garlic powder and pepper. Spread onto the cauliflower. Serve immediately.

Nutrition Info per Serving:
calories: 278 | fat: 15g | protein: 14g | carbs: 16g | net carbs: 8g | sugar: 9.4g | fibre: 8g

Golden Biscuits

Prep time: 15 minutes | Cook time: 13 minutes | Serves 8

190 g blanched almond flour
10 g sweetener
1 tsp. baking powder
½ tsp. fine sea salt
55 g plus 2 tbsps. very cold unsalted butter
60 ml unsweetened,
unflavoured almond milk
1 large egg
1 tsp. vanilla extract
3 tsps. ground cinnamon
Glaze:
10 g sweetener
60 g heavy cream

1. Preheat the air fryer to 180ºC. Line a pie pan that fits into your air fryer with parchment paper.
2. In a medium-sized bowl, mix together the almond flour, sweetener (if powdered, do not add liquid sweetener), baking powder, and salt. Cut the butter into 1-cm squares, and then use a hand mixer to work the butter into the dry ingredients. When you are done, the mixture should still have chunks of butter.
3. In a small bowl, whisk together the almond milk, egg, and vanilla extract (if using liquid sweetener, add it as well) until blended. Using a fork, stir the wet ingredients into the dry ingredients until large clumps form. Add the cinnamon and use your hands to swirl it into the dough.
4. Form the dough into sixteen 2-cm balls and place them on the prepared pan, spacing them about 1-cm apart. (If you're using a smaller air fryer, work in batches if necessary.) Bake in the air fryer until golden, for 10 to 13 minutes. Remove from the air fryer and let it cool on the pan for at least 5 minutes.
5. While the biscuits bake, make the glaze: Place the powdered sweetener in a small bowl and slowly stir in the heavy cream with a fork.
6. When the biscuits have cooled somewhat, dip the tops into the glaze, allow it to dry a bit, and then dip again for a thick glaze.
7. Serve warm or at room temperature. Store unglazed biscuits in an airtight container in the refrigerator for up to 3 days or in the freezer for up to a month. Reheat in a preheated 180ºC air fryer for 5 minutes, or until warmed through, and dip in the glaze as instructed above.

Nutrition Info per Serving:
calories: 546 | fat: 51g | protein: 14g | carbs: 13g | net carbs: 7g | sugar: 17.5g | fibre: 6g

Bacon Lettuce Wraps, page 14

Blueberry Muffin, page 14

Broccoli and Mushroom Frittata, page 14

Cauliflower Hash Browns, page 18

Sausage Egg Cup, page 15

Ham Egg, page 19

Chapter 3 Breakfast 17

Cauliflower Hash Browns

Prep time: 20 minutes | Cook time: 12 minutes | Serves 4

1 (340-g) steamer bag cauliflower
1 large egg
100 g shredded sharp Cheddar cheese

1. Place the bag in microwave and cook according to package instructions. Allow it to cool completely and put cauliflower into a cheesecloth or kitchen towel and squeeze to remove excess moisture.
2. Mash cauliflower with a fork and add egg and cheese.
3. Cut a piece of parchment to fit your air fryer basket. Take ¼ of the mixture and form it into a hash brown patty shape. Place it onto the parchment and into the air fryer basket, working in batches if necessary.
4. Adjust the temperature to 205ºC and set the timer for 12 minutes.
5. Flip the hash browns halfway through the cooking time. When completely cooked, they will be golden brown. Serve immediately.

Nutrition Info per Serving:
calories: 153 | fat: 9g | protein: 10g | carbs: 5g | net carbs: 3g | sugar: 7g | fibre: 2g

Sausage with Peppers

Prep time: 15 minutes | Cook time: 15 minutes | Serves 4

230 g spicy pork sausage meat
4 large eggs
115 g full-fat cream cheese, softened
60 g canned diced tomatoes and green chilies, drained
4 large poblano peppers
8 tbsps. shredded pepper jack cheese
115 g full-fat sour cream

1. In a medium skillet over medium heat, crumble and brown the sausage until no pink remains. Remove sausage and drain the fat from the pan. Crack eggs into the pan, scramble, and cook until no longer runny.
2. Place the cooked sausage in a large bowl and fold in cream cheese. Mix in diced tomatoes and chilies. Gently fold in eggs.
3. Cut a 8-cm–10-cm slit in the top of each poblano, removing the seeds and white membrane with a small knife. Separate the filling into four servings and spoon carefully into each pepper. Top each with 2 tbsps. pepper jack cheese.
4. Place each pepper into the air fryer basket.
5. Adjust the temperature to 180ºC and set the timer for 15 minutes.
6. Peppers will be soft and cheese will be browned when ready. Serve immediately with sour cream on top.

Nutrition Info per Serving:
calories: 489 | fat: 35g | protein: 23g | carbs: 13g | net carbs: 9g | sugar: 13.1g | fibre: 4g

Broccoli Frittata

Prep time: 15 minutes | Cook time: 12 minutes | Serves 4

6 large eggs
60 g heavy whipping cream
50 g chopped broccoli
20 g chopped yellow onion
30 g chopped green pepper

1. In a large bowl, whisk eggs and heavy whipping cream. Mix in broccoli, onion, and pepper.
2. Pour into a 12-cm round oven-safe baking dish. Place baking dish into the air fryer basket.
3. Adjust the temperature to 180ºC and set the timer for 12 minutes.
4. Eggs should be firm and cooked fully when the frittata is done. Serve warm.

Nutrition Info per Serving:
calories: 168 | fat: 11g | protein: 10g | carbs: 3g | net carbs: 2g | sugar: 5.7g | fibre: 1g

Egg with Cheddar

Prep time: 5 minutes | Cook time: 15 minutes | Serves 2

4 large eggs
2 tbsps. unsalted butter, melted
50 g shredded sharp Cheddar cheese

1. Crack eggs into a round baking dish and whisk. Place dish into the air fryer basket.
2. Adjust the temperature to 205°C and set the timer for 10 minutes.
3. After 5 minutes, stir the eggs and add the butter and cheese. Cook for 3 more minutes and stir again.
4. Allow the eggs to finish cooking for an additional 2 minutes or remove if they are to your desired liking.
5. Use a fork to fluff. Serve warm.

Nutrition Info per Serving:
calories: 359 | fat: 27g | protein: 20g | carbs: 1g | net carbs: 1g | sugar: 8.6g | fibre: 0g

Spinach Omelet

Prep time: 5 minutes | Cook time: 12 minutes | Serves 2

4 large eggs
45 g chopped fresh spinach leaves
2 tbsps. peeled and chopped yellow onion
2 tbsps. salted butter, melted
50 g shredded mild Cheddar cheese
¼ tsp. salt

1. In an ungreased 12-cm round nonstick baking dish, whisk eggs. Stir in spinach, onion, butter, Cheddar, and salt.
2. Place dish into air fryer basket. Adjust the temperature to 160ºC and set the timer for 12 minutes. Omelet will be done when browned on the top and firm in the middle.
3. Slice in half and serve warm on two medium plates.

Nutrition Info per Serving:
calories: 368 | fat: 28g | protein: 20g | carbs: 3g | net carbs: 2g | sugar: 5.3g | fibre: 1g

Chocolate Chip Muffin

Prep time: 5 minutes | Cook time: 15 minutes | Makes 6 muffins

145 g blanched finely ground almond flour
15 g granulated sweetener
4 tbsps. salted butter, melted
2 large eggs, whisked
1 tbsp. baking powder
85 g low-carb chocolate chips

1. In a large bowl, combine all ingredients. Evenly pour batter into six silicone muffin cups greased with cooking spray.
2. Place muffin cups into air fryer basket. Adjust the temperature to 160ºC and set the timer for 15 minutes. Muffins will be golden brown when done.
3. Let the muffins cool in cups for 15 minutes to avoid crumbling. Serve warm.

Nutrition Info per Serving:
calories: 329 | fat: 29g | protein: 10g | carbs: 28g | net carbs: 20g | sugar: 14g | fibre: 8g

Ham Egg

Prep time: 10 minutes | Cook time: 15 minutes | Serves 4

4 medium green peppers, tops removed, seeded
1 tbsp. coconut oil
85 g chopped cooked ham
15 g peeled and chopped white onion
4 large eggs
½ tsp. salt
100 g shredded mild Cheddar cheese

1. Place peppers upright into ungreased air fryer basket. Drizzle each pepper with coconut oil. Divide ham and onion evenly among peppers.
2. In a medium bowl, whisk eggs, then sprinkle with salt. Pour mixture evenly into each pepper. Top each with 25 g Cheddar.
3. Adjust the temperature to 160ºC and set the timer for 15 minutes. Peppers will be tender and eggs will be firm when done.
4. Serve warm on four medium plates.

Nutrition Info per Serving:
calories: 281 | fat: 18g | protein: 18g | carbs: 8g | net carbs: 6g | sugar: 5.9g | fibre: 2g

Spinach and Tomato Egg

Prep time: 10 minutes | Cook time: 15 minutes | Serves 4

485 g 100% liquid egg whites
3 tbsps. salted butter, melted
¼ tsp. salt
¼ tsp. onion powder
½ medium Roma tomato, cored and diced
15 g chopped fresh spinach leaves

1. In a large bowl, whisk egg whites with butter, salt, and onion powder. Stir in tomato and spinach, then pour evenly into four 8-cm ramekins greased with cooking spray.
2. Place ramekins into air fryer basket. Adjust the temperature to 150°C and set the timer for 15 minutes. Eggs will be fully cooked and firm in the centre when done. Serve warm.

Nutrition Info per Serving:
calories: 146 | fat: 8g | protein: 14g | carbs: 1g | net carbs: 1g | sugar: 1.5g | fibre: 0g

Pepperoni Egg

Prep time: 5 minutes | Cook time: 10 minutes | Serves 2

85 g shredded Mozzarella cheese
7 slices pepperoni, chopped
1 large egg, whisked
¼ tsp. dried oregano
¼ tsp. dried parsley
¼ tsp. garlic powder
¼ tsp. salt

1. Place Mozzarella in a single layer on the bottom of an ungreased 12-cm round nonstick baking dish. Scatter pepperoni over cheese, then pour egg evenly around baking dish.
2. Sprinkle with the remaining ingredients and place into air fryer basket. Adjust the temperature to 165ºC and set the timer for 10 minutes. When cheese is brown and egg is set, dish will be done.
3. Let it cool in dish 5 minutes before serving.

Nutrition Info per Serving:
calories: 241 | fat: 15g | protein: 19g | carbs: 4g | net carbs: 4g | sugar: 4.2g | fibre: 0g

Chapter 4 Vegetable and Meatless

Super Cheese Cauliflower Fritters

Prep time: 15 minutes | Cook time: 10 minutes | Serves 8

910 g cauliflower florets
30 g spring onions, finely chopped
½ tsp. freshly ground black pepper, or more to taste
1 tbsp. fine sea salt
½ tsp. hot paprika
195 g cheddar cheese, shredded
100 g Parmesan cheese, grated
60 ml olive oil

1. Firstly, boil the cauliflower until fork tender. Drain, peel and mash your cauliflower.
2. Thoroughly mix the mashed cauliflower with spring onions, pepper, salt, paprika, and Colby cheese. Then, shape the balls using your hands. Now, flatten the balls to make the patties.
3. Roll the patties over grated Parmesan cheese. Drizzle olive oil over them.
4. Next, cook your patties at 180ºC approximately 10 minutes, working in batches. Serve with tabasco mayo if desired. Bon appétit!

Nutrition Info per Serving:
calories: 282 | fat: 22g | protein: 13g | carbs: 8g | net carbs: 6g | sugar: 13.4g | fibre: 2g

Cheese-Broccoli Fritters

Prep time: 10 minutes | Cook time: 25 minutes | Serves 4

90 g broccoli florets
85 g shredded Mozzarella cheese
75 g almond flour
50 g flaxseed meal, divided
2 tsps. baking powder
1 tsp. garlic powder
Salt and freshly ground black pepper
2 eggs, lightly beaten
120 ml ranch dressing

1. Preheat the air fryer to 205°C.
2. In a food processor fitted with a metal blade, pulse the broccoli until very finely chopped.
3. Transfer the broccoli to a large bowl and add the Mozzarella, almond flour, 25 g of the flaxseed meal, baking powder, and garlic powder. Stir until thoroughly combined. Season to taste with salt and black pepper. Add the eggs and stir again to form a sticky dough. Shape the dough into 1/2-cm fritters.
4. Place the remaining flaxseed meal in a shallow bowl and roll the fritters in the meal to form an even coating.
5. Working in batches if necessary, arrange the fritters in a single layer in the basket of the air fryer and spray generously with olive oil. Pausing halfway through the cooking time to shake the basket, air fry for 20 to 25 minutes until the fritters are golden brown and crispy. Serve with the ranch dressing for dipping.

Nutrition Info per Serving:
calories: 450 | fat: 36g | protein: 19g | carbs: 16g | net carbs: 10g | sugar: 5.6g | fibre: 6g

Aubergine Lasagna

Prep time: 15 minutes | Cook time: 36 minutes | Serves 4

1 small aubergine (about 340 g), sliced into rounds
2 tsps. salt
1 tbsp. olive oil
110 g shredded Mozzarella, divided
245 g ricotta cheese
1 large egg
25 g grated Parmesan cheese
½ tsp. dried oregano
395 g no-sugar-added marinara
1 tbsp. chopped fresh parsley

1. Preheat the air fryer to 180ºC. Coat a casserole dish that fits in your air fryer with olive oil, set aside.
2. Arrange the aubergine slices in a single layer on a baking sheet and sprinkle with the salt. Let sit for 10 minutes. Use a paper towel to remove the excess moisture and salt.
3. Working in batches if necessary, brush the aubergine with the olive oil and arrange in a single layer in the air fryer basket. Pausing halfway through the cooking time to turn the aubergine, air fry for 6 minutes until softened. Transfer the aubergine back to the baking sheet and let it cool.
4. In a small bowl, combine 55 g of the Mozzarella with the ricotta, egg, Parmesan, and oregano. To assemble the lasagna, spread a spoonful of marinara in the bottom of the casserole dish, followed by a layer of aubergine, a layer of the cheese mixture, and a layer of marinara. Repeat the layers until all of the ingredients are used, ending with the remaining 55 g of Mozzarella. Scatter the parsley on top. Cover the baking dish with foil.
5. Increase the air fryer to 190ºC and air fry for 30 minutes. Uncover the dish and continue baking for 10 minutes longer until the cheese begins to brown. Let the casserole sit for at least 10 minutes before serving.

Nutrition Info per Serving:
calories: 350 | fat: 22g | protein: 20g | carbs: 17g | net carbs: 12g | sugar: 8g | fibre: 5g

Cheddar Green Beans

Prep time: 15 minutes | Cook time: 15 minutes | Serves 3

230 g green beans
255 g Cheddar cheese, sliced
55 g tomato paste, no sugar added
1 tbsp. white vinegar
1 tbsp. mustard
¼ tsp. ground black pepper
½ tsp. sea salt
¼ tsp. smoked paprika
½ tsp. freshly grated ginger
2 cloves garlic, minced
2 tbsps. olive oil

1. Toss green beans with the tomato paste, white vinegar, mustard, black pepper, sea salt, paprika, ginger, garlic, and olive oil.
2. Cook at 200ºC in the air fryer for 10 minutes. Top with Cheddar cheese and cook for an additional 5 minutes or until cheese melts.
3. Serve immediately. Bon appétit!

Nutrition Info per Serving:
calories: 455 | fat: 38g | protein: 22.1g | carbs: 7.7g | net carbs: 6.3g | sugar: 1.1g | fibre: 2.3g

Asparagus with Broccoli

Prep time: 25 minutes | Cook time: 22 minutes | Serves 4

230g asparagus, cut into 1-cm pieces
230g broccoli, cut into 1-cm pieces
2 tbsps. olive oil
Some salt and white pepper, to taste
120 ml vegetable stock
2 tbsps. apple cider vinegar

1. Place the vegetables in a single layer in the lightly greased cooking basket. Drizzle the olive oil over the vegetables.
2. Sprinkle with salt and white pepper.
3. Cook at 190ºC for 15 minutes, shaking the basket halfway through the cooking time.
4. Add 120 ml of vegetable stock to a saucepan, bring to a rapid boil and add the vinegar. Cook for 5 to 7 minutes or until the sauce has reduced by half.
5. Spoon the sauce over the warm vegetables and serve immediately. Bon appétit!

Nutrition Info per Serving:
calories: 181 | fat: 7g | protein: 3g | carbs: 4g | net carbs: 1g | sugar: 0g | fibre: 3g

Tofu with Chili-Galirc Sauce

Prep time: 10 minutes | Cook time: 20 minutes | Serves 4

1 (455-g) block extra-firm tofu
2 tbsps. coconut aminos
1 tbsp. toasted sesame oil
1 tbsp. olive oil
1 tbsp. chili-garlic sauce
1½ tsps. black sesame seeds
1 spring onion, thinly sliced

1. Press the tofu for at least 15 minutes by wrapping it in paper towels and setting a heavy pan on top so that the moisture drains.
2. Slice the tofu into bite-size cubes and transfer to a bowl. Drizzle with the coconut aminos, sesame oil, olive oil, and chili-garlic sauce. Cover and refrigerate for 1 hour or up to overnight.
3. Preheat the air fryer to 205°C.
4. Arrange the tofu in a single layer in the air fryer basket. Pausing to shake the pan halfway through the cooking time, air fry for 15 to 20 minutes until crisp. Serve with any juices that accumulate in the bottom of the air fryer, sprinkled with the sesame seeds and sliced spring onion.

Nutrition Info per Serving:
calories: 180 | fat: 13g | protein: 11g | carbs: 5g | net carbs: 4g | sugar: 0.5g | fibre: 1g

Courgette and Mushroom Kebab

Prep time: 40 minutes | Cook time: 8 minutes | Makes 8 skewers

1 medium courgette, trimmed and cut into 1-cm slices
½ medium yellow onion, peeled and cut into 2-cm squares
1 medium red pepper, seeded and cut into 2-cm squares
16 whole cremini mushrooms
70 g basil pesto
½ tsp. salt
¼ tsp. ground black pepper

1. Divide courgette slices, onion, and pepper into eight even portions. Place on 12-cm skewers for a total of eight kebabs. Add 2 mushrooms to each skewer and brush kebabs generously with pesto.
2. Sprinkle each kebab with salt and black pepper on all sides, then place into ungreased air fryer basket. Adjust the temperature to 190ºC and set the timer for 8 minutes, turning kebabs halfway through cooking. Vegetables will be browned at the edges and tender-crisp when done. Serve warm.

Nutrition Info per Serving:
calories: 107 | fat: 7g | protein: 4g | carbs: 10g | net carbs: 8g | sugar: 0.5g | fibre: 2g

Broccoli Croquettes

Prep time: 15 minutes | Cook time: 10 minutes | Serves 4

230 g broccoli florets
1 tbsp. ground flaxseeds
1 yellow onion, finely chopped
1 pepper, seeded and chopped
2 garlic cloves, pressed
1 tsp. turmeric powder
½ tsp. ground cumin
50 g almond flour
50 g Parmesan cheese
2 eggs, whisked
Salt and ground black pepper, to taste
2 tbsps. olive oil

1. Blanch the broccoli in salted boiling water until al-dente, for about 3 to 4 minutes. Drain well and transfer to a mixing bowl, mash the broccoli florets with the remaining ingredients.
2. Form the mixture into patties and place them in the lightly greased Air Fryer basket.
3. Cook at 205ºC for 6 minutes, turning them over halfway through the cooking time, work in batches.
4. Serve warm with mayonnaise. Enjoy!

Nutrition Info per Serving:
calories: 219 | fat: 16.6g | protein: 10g | carbs: 6.5g | net carbs: 5g | sugar: 1g | fibre: 3.2g

Spinach Cheese Casserole

Prep time: 15 minutes | Cook time: 15 minutes | Serves 4

1 tbsp. salted butter, melted
15 g diced yellow onion
230 g full-fat cream cheese, softened
65 g full-fat mayonnaise
70 g full-fat sour cream
25 g chopped pickled jalapeños
60 g fresh spinach, chopped
215 g cauliflower florets, chopped
175 g artichoke hearts, chopped

1. In a large bowl, mix butter, onion, cream cheese, mayonnaise, and sour cream. Fold in jalapeños, spinach, cauliflower, and artichokes.
2. Pour the mixture into a round baking dish. Cover with foil and place into the air fryer basket.
3. Adjust the temperature to 190ºC and set the timer for 15 minutes.
4. In the last 2 minutes of cooking, remove the foil to brown the top. Serve warm.

Nutrition Info per Serving:
calories: 423 | fat: 36.3g | protein: 6.7g | carbs: 12.1g | net carbs: 6.8g | sugar: 9.3g | fibre: 5.3g

Cheese Stuffed Pepper

Prep time: 20 minutes | Cook time: 15 minutes | Serves 2

1 red pepper, top and seeds removed
1 yellow pepper, top and seeds removed
Salt and pepper, to taste
225 g Cottage cheese
4 tbsps. mayonnaise
2 pickles, chopped

1. Arrange the peppers in the lightly greased cooking basket. Cook in the preheated Air Fryer at 205ºC for 15 minutes, turning them over halfway through the cooking time.
2. Season with salt and pepper.
3. Then, in a mixing bowl, combine the cream cheese with the mayonnaise and chopped pickles. Stuff the pepper with the cream cheese mixture and serve. Enjoy!

Nutrition Info per Serving:
calories: 360 | fat: 27.3g | protein: 20.3g | carbs: 7.6g | net carbs: 6.4g | sugar: 7.2g | fibre: 1.2g

Aubergine with Tomato and Cheese

Prep time: 35 minutes | Cook time: 5 minutes | Serves 4

1 aubergine, peeled and sliced
2 peppers, seeded and sliced
1 red onion, sliced
1 tsp. fresh garlic, minced
4 tbsps. olive oil
1 tsp. mustard
1 tsp. dried oregano
1 tsp. smoked paprika
Salt and ground black pepper, to taste
1 tomato, sliced
170 g halloumi cheese, sliced lengthways

1. Start by preheating your Air Fryer to 190ºC. Spritz a baking pan with nonstick cooking spray.
2. Place the aubergine, peppers, onion, and garlic on the bottom of the baking pan. Add the olive oil, mustard, and spices. Transfer to the cooking basket and cook for 14 minutes.
3. Top with the tomatoes and cheese, increase the temperature to 200ºC and cook for 5 minutes or more until bubbling. Let it sit on a cooling rack for 10 minutes before serving.
4. Bon appétit!

Nutrition Info per Serving:
calories: 306 | fat: 16.1g | protein: 39.6g | carbs: 8.8g | net carbs: 7g | sugar: 6.4g | fibre: 1.8g

Broccoli with Herbed Garlic Sauce, page 28

Courgette and Mushroom Kebab, page 23

Broccoli Croquettes, page 24

Aubergine Lasagna, page 22

Mushroom Soufflés, page 26

Spinach Cheese Casserole, page 24

Chapter 4 Vegetable and Meatless   25

Courgette with Spinach

Prep time: 9 minutes | Cook time: 7 minutes | Serves 6

4 eggs, slightly beaten
50 g almond flour
180 g goat cheese, crumbled
1 tsp. fine sea salt
4 garlic cloves, minced
30 g baby spinach
50 g Parmesan cheese grated
⅓ tsp. red pepper flakes
455 g courgette, peeled and grated
⅓ tsp. dried dill weed

1. Thoroughly combine all ingredients in a bowl. Now, roll the mixture to form small croquettes.
2. Air fry at 170ºC for 7 minutes or until golden. Tate, adjust for seasonings and serve warm.

Nutrition Info per Serving:
calories: 171 | fat: 10.8g | protein: 3.1g | carbs: 15.9g | net carbs: 14.9g | sugar: 5g | fibre: 1g

Cauliflower with Cheese

Prep time: 15 minutes | Cook time: 30 minutes | Serves 4

535 g cauliflower florets
65 g almond flour
½ tsp. salt
55 g unsalted butter, melted
25 g grated Parmesan cheese

1. In a food processor fitted with a metal blade, pulse the cauliflower until finely chopped. Transfer the cauliflower to a large microwave-safe bowl and cover it with a paper towel. Microwave for 5 minutes. Spread the cauliflower on a towel to cool.
2. When cool enough to handle, draw up the sides of the towel and squeeze tightly over a sink to remove the excess moisture. Return the cauliflower to the food processor and whirl until creamy. Sprinkle the flour and salt and pulse until a sticky dough comes together.
3. Transfer the dough to a workspace lightly floured with almond flour. Shape the dough into a ball and divide into 4 equal sections. Roll each section into a rope 2-cm thick. Slice the dough into squares with a sharp knife.
4. Preheat the air fryer to 205°C.
5. Working in batches if necessary, place the gnocchi in a single layer in the basket of the air fryer and spray generously with olive oil. Pausing halfway through the cooking time to turn the gnocchi, air fry for 25 to 30 minutes until golden brown and crispy on the edges. Transfer to a large bowl and toss with the melted butter and Parmesan cheese.

Nutrition Info per Serving:
calories: 360 | fat: 20g | protein: 9g | carbs: 14g | net carbs: 10g | sugar: 7.6g | fibre: 4g

Riced Cauliflower with Eggs

Prep time: 10 minutes | Cook time: 12 minutes | Serves 4

215 g cauliflower, food-processed into rice-like particles
2 tbsps. peanut oil
30 g spring onions, chopped
2 peppers, chopped
4 eggs, beaten
Sea salt and ground black pepper, to taste
½ tsp. granulated garlic

1. Grease a baking pan with nonstick cooking spray.
2. Add the cauliflower rice and the other ingredients to the baking pan.
3. Cook at 205ºC for 12 minutes, checking occasionally to ensure even cooking. Enjoy!

Nutrition Info per Serving:
calories: 149 | fat: 11g | protein: 2.4g | carbs: 6.1g | net carbs: 4.5g | sugar: 0.6g | fibre: 1.7g

Mushroom Soufflés

Prep time: 15 minutes | Cook time: 12 minutes | Serves 4

3 large eggs, whites and yolks separated
55 g sharp white Cheddar cheese
85 g cream cheese, softened
¼ tsp. cream of tartar
¼ tsp. salt
¼ tsp. ground black pepper
35 g cremini mushrooms, sliced

1. In a large bowl, whip egg whites until stiff peaks form, for about 2 minutes. In a separate large bowl, beat Cheddar, egg yolks, cream cheese, cream of tartar, salt, and pepper together until combined.
2. Fold egg whites into cheese mixture, being careful not to stir. Fold in mushrooms, then pour mixture evenly into four ungreased 8-cramekins.
3. Place ramekins into air fryer basket. Adjust the temperature to 175°C and set the timer for 12 minutes. Eggs will be browned on the top and firm in the centre when done. Serve warm.

Nutrition Info per Serving:
calories: 185 | fat: 14g | protein: 10g | carbs: 2g | net carbs: 2g | sugar: 9g | fibre: 0g

Roast Aubergine and Courgette Bites

Prep time: 35 minutes | Cook time: 30 minutes | Serves 8

2 tsps. fresh mint leaves, chopped
1½ tsps. red pepper chili flakes
2 tbsps. melted butter
455 g aubergine, peeled and cubed
455 g Courgette, peeled and cubed
3 tbsps. olive oil

1. Toss all of the above ingredients in a large-sized mixing dish.
2. Roast the aubergine and Courgette bites for 30 minutes at 160ºC in your Air Fryer, turning once or twice.
3. Serve with a homemade dipping sauce.

Nutrition Info per Serving:
calories: 110 | fat: 8.3g | protein: 2.6g | carbs: 8.8g | net carbs: 6.3g | sugar: 0.2g | fibre: 2.5g

Citrus Courgette Balls

Prep time: 5 minutes | Cook time: 15 minutes | Serves 4

455 g courgette, grated
1 tbsp. orange juice
½ tsp. ground cinnamon
¼ tsp. ground cloves
50 g almond flour
1 tsp. baking powder
80 g coconut flakes

1. In a mixing bowl, thoroughly combine all ingredients, except for coconut flakes.
2. Roll the balls in the coconut flakes.
3. Bake in the preheated Air Fryer at 180ºC for 15 minutes or until thoroughly cooked and crispy.
4. Repeat the process until you run out of ingredients. Bon appétit!

Nutrition Info per Serving:
calories: 166 | fat: 13.1g | protein: 6.2g | carbs: 9.6g | net carbs: 7g | sugar: 0.1g | fibre: 4.7g

Mushroom with Artichoke and Spinach

Prep time: 10 minutes | Cook time: 14 minutes | Serves 4

2 tbsps. olive oil
4 large portobello mushrooms, stems removed and gills scraped out
½ tsp. salt
¼ tsp. freshly ground pepper
115 g goat cheese, crumbled
85 g chopped marinated artichoke hearts
30 g frozen spinach, thawed and squeezed dry
50 g grated Parmesan cheese
2 tbsps. chopped fresh parsley

1. Preheat the air fryer to 205°C.
2. Rub the olive oil over the portobello mushrooms until thoroughly coated. Sprinkle both sides with the salt and black pepper. Place top-side down on a clean work surface.
3. In a small bowl, combine the goat cheese, artichoke hearts, and spinach. Mash with the back of a fork until thoroughly combined. Divide the cheese mixture among the mushrooms and sprinkle with the Parmesan cheese.
4. Air fry for 10 to 14 minutes until the mushrooms are tender and the cheese has begun to brown. Top with the fresh parsley just before serving.

Nutrition Info per Serving:
calories: 270 | fat: 23g | protein: 8g | carbs: 11g | net carbs: 7g | sugar: 6.5g | fibre: 4g

Broccoli with Herbed Garlic Sauce

Prep time: 19 minutes | Cook time: 15 minutes | Serves 4

2 tbsps. olive oil
Salt and freshly ground black pepper, to taste
455 g broccoli florets
For the Dipping Sauce:
2 tsps. dried rosemary, crushed

3 garlic cloves, minced
⅓ tsp. dried marjoram, crushed
60 g sour cream
65 g mayonnaise

1. Lightly grease your broccoli with a thin layer of olive oil. Season with salt and ground black pepper.
2. Arrange the seasoned broccoli in an Air Fryer cooking basket. Bake at 200ºC for 15 minutes, shaking once or twice.
3. In the meantime, prepare the dipping sauce by mixing all the sauce ingredients. Serve warm broccoli with the dipping sauce and enjoy!

Nutrition Info per Serving:
calories: 247 | fat: 22g | protein: 4g | carbs: 9g | net carbs: 6g | sugar: 5.1g | fibre: 3g

Cheese Stuffed Courgette

Prep time: 20 minutes | Cook time: 8 minutes | Serves 4

1 large courgette, cut into four pieces
2 tbsps. olive oil
250 g Ricotta cheese, room temperature
2 tbsps. spring onions, chopped
1 heaping tbsp. fresh parsley, roughly chopped

1 heaping tbsp. coriander, minced
60 g Cheddar cheese, preferably freshly grated
1 tsp. celery seeds
½ tsp. salt
½ tsp. garlic pepper

1. Cook your courgette in the Air Fryer cooking basket for approximately 10 minutes at 180ºC. Check for doneness and cook for 2-3 minutes longer if needed.
2. Meanwhile, make the stuffing by mixing the other items.
3. When your courgette is thoroughly cooked, open them up. Divide the stuffing among all courgette pieces and bake for an additional 5 minutes.

Nutrition Info per Serving:
calories: 199 | fat: 16.4g | protein: 9.2g | carbs: 4.5g | net carbs: 4g | sugar: 8.3g | fibre: 0.5g

Chapter 5 Meat and Poultry

Ham Chicken with Cheese

Prep time: 15 minutes | Cook time: 25 minutes | Serves 4

55 g unsalted butter, softened	60 ml water
115 g cream cheese, softened	280 g shredded cooked chicken
1½ tsps. Dijon mustard	115 g ham, chopped
2 tbsps. white wine vinegar	115 g sliced Swiss or Provolone cheese

1. Preheat the air fryer to 190ºC. Lightly coat a casserole dish that will fit in the air fryer, such as an 16-cm round pan, with olive oil and set aside.
2. In a large bowl and using an electric mixer, combine the butter, cream cheese, Dijon mustard, and vinegar. With the motor running on low speed, slowly add the water and beat until smooth. Set aside.
3. Arrange an even layer of chicken in the bottom of the prepared pan, followed by the ham. Spread the butter and cream cheese mixture on top of the ham, followed by the cheese slices on the top layer. Air fry for 20 to 25 minutes until warmed through and the cheese has browned.

Nutrition Info per Serving:
calories: 480 | fat: 36g | protein: 34g | carbs: 4g | net carbs: 4g | sugar: 12g | fibre: 0g

Lime Marinated Lamb Chop

Prep time: 5 minutes | Cook time: 5 minutes | Serves 2

4 (2-cm thick) lamb chops	60 ml avocado oil
Sprigs of fresh mint, for garnish (optional)	15 g chopped fresh mint leaves
Lime slices, for serving (optional)	4 cloves garlic, roughly chopped
Marinade:	2 tsps. fine sea salt
2 tsps. grated lime zest	½ tsp. ground black pepper
120 ml lime juice	

1. Make the marinade: Place all the ingredients for the marinade in a food processor or blender and purée until mostly smooth with a few small chunks. Transfer half of the marinade to a shallow dish and set the other half aside for serving. Add the lamb to the shallow dish, cover, and place in the refrigerator to marinate for at least 2 hours or overnight.
2. Spray the air fryer basket with avocado oil. Preheat the air fryer to 200ºC.
3. Remove the chops from the marinade and place them in the air fryer basket. Cook for 5 minutes, or until the internal temperature reaches 60°C for medium doneness.
4. Allow the chops to rest for 10 minutes before serving with the rest of the marinade as a sauce. Garnish with fresh mint leaves and serve with lime slices, if desired. Best served fresh.

Nutrition Info per Serving:
calories: 692 | fat: 53g | protein: 48g | carbs: 2g | net carbs: 1g | sugar: 0.5g | fibre: 1g

Skirt Steak Carne Asada

Prep time: 5 minutes | Cook time: 8 minutes | Serves 4

Marinade:	1 tsp. stevia glycerite
60 g fresh coriander leaves and stems, plus more for garnish if desired	2 tsps. ancho chili powder
	2 tsps. fine sea salt
1 jalapeño pepper, seeded and diced	1 tsp. coriander seeds
	1 tsp. cumin seeds
120 ml lime juice	455 g skirt steak, cut into 4 equal portions
2 tbsps. avocado oil	**For Serving (Optional):**
2 tbsps. coconut vinegar or apple cider vinegar	Chopped avocado
	Lime slices
2 tsps. orange extract	Sliced radishes

1. Make the marinade: Place all the ingredients for the marinade in a blender and puree until smooth.
2. Place the steak in a shallow dish and pour the marinade over it, making sure the meat is covered completely. Cover and place in the fridge for 2 hours or overnight.
3. Spray the air fryer basket with avocado oil. Preheat the air fryer to 205°C..
4. Remove the steak from the marinade and place it in the air fryer basket in one layer. Cook for 8 minutes, or until the internal temperature is 60°C, do not overcook or it will become tough.
5. Remove the steak from the air fryer and place it on a cutting board to rest for 10 minutes before slicing it against the grain. Garnish with coriander, if desired, and serve with chopped avocado, lime slices, and/or sliced radishes, if desired.
6. Store the leftovers in an airtight container in the fridge for 3 days or in the freezer for up to a month. Reheat in a preheated 175°C air fryer for 4 minutes, or until heated through.

Nutrition Info per Serving:
calories: 265 | fat: 17g | protein: 24g | carbs: 4g | net carbs: 3g | sugar: 0.5g | fibre: 1g

Pork Tenderloin with Ricotta

Prep time: 25 minutes | Cook time: 22 minutes | Serves 4

2 tbsps. olive oil
910 g pork tenderloin, cut into serving-size pieces
1 tsp. coarse sea salt
½ tsp. freshly ground pepper
¼ tsp. chili powder
1 tsp. dried marjoram
1 tbsp. mustard
250 g Ricotta cheese
360 ml chicken stock

1. Start by preheating your Air Fryer to 180ºC.
2. Heat the olive oil in a pan over medium-high heat. Once hot, cook the pork for 6 to 7 minutes, flipping it to ensure even cooking.
3. Arrange the pork in a lightly greased casserole dish. Season with salt, black pepper, chili powder, and marjoram.
4. In a mixing dish, thoroughly combine the mustard, cheese, and chicken stock. Pour the mixture over the pork chops in the casserole dish.
5. Bake for another 15 minutes or until bubbly and heated through. Bon appétit!

Nutrition Info per Serving:
calories: 433 | fat: 20g | protein: 56g | carbs: 3g | net carbs: 2g | sugar: 7g | fibre: 1g

Pork Cutlets with Red Wine

Prep time: 20 minutes | Cook time: 15 minutes | Serves 2

240 ml water
240 ml red wine
1 tbsp. sea salt
2 pork cutlets
25 g almond flour
30 g flaxseed meal
½ tsp. baking powder
1 tsp. shallot powder
½ tsp. porcini powder
Sea salt and ground black pepper, to taste
1 egg
60 g yogurt
1 tsp. brown mustard
30 g Parmesan cheese, grated

1. In a large ceramic dish, combine the water, wine and salt. Add the pork cutlets and put for 1 hour in the refrigerator.
2. In a shallow bowl, mix the almond flour, flaxseed meal, baking powder, shallot powder, porcini powder, salt, and ground pepper. In another bowl, whisk the eggs with yogurt and mustard.
3. In a third bowl, place the grated Parmesan cheese.
4. Dip the pork cutlets in the seasoned flour mixture and toss evenly, then, in the egg mixture. Finally, roll them over the grated Parmesan cheese.
5. Spritz the bottom of the cooking basket with cooking oil. Add the breaded pork cutlets and cook at 200ºC and for 10 minutes.
6. Flip and cook for 5 minutes or more on the other side. Serve warm.

Nutrition Info per Serving:
calories: 450 | fat: 26g | protein: 41g | carbs: 9g | net carbs: 7g | sugar: 6.2g | fibre: 2g

Herbed Lamb Chops with Parmesan

Prep time: 10 minutes | Cook time: 5 minutes | Serves 2

1 large egg
2 cloves garlic, minced
25 g powdered Parmesan cheese
1 tbsp. chopped fresh oregano leaves
1 tbsp. chopped fresh rosemary leaves
1 tsp. chopped fresh thyme leaves
½ tsp. ground black pepper
4 (2-cm-thick) lamb chops
For Garnish/Serving (Optional):
Sprigs of fresh oregano
Sprigs of fresh rosemary
Sprigs of fresh thyme
Lavender flowers
Lemon slices

1. Spray the air fryer basket with avocado oil. Preheat the air fryer to 205°C..
2. Beat the egg in a shallow bowl, add the garlic, and stir well to combine. In another shallow bowl, mix together Parmesan, herbs, and pepper.
3. One at a time, dip the lamb chops into the egg mixture, shake off the excess egg, and then dredge them in the Parmesan mixture. Use your hands to coat the chops well in the Parmesan mixture and form a nice crust on all sides, if necessary, dip the chops again in both the egg and the Parmesan mixture.
4. Place the lamb chops in the air fryer basket, leaving space between them, and cook for 5 minutes, or until the internal temperature reaches 60°C for medium doneness. Allow them to rest for 10 minutes before serving.
5. Garnish with sprigs of oregano, rosemary, and thyme, and lavender flowers, if desired. Serve with lemon slices, if desired.
6. Best served fresh. Store leftovers in an airtight container in the fridge for up to 4 days. Serve chilled over a salad, or reheat in a 175°C air fryer for 3 minutes, or until heated through.

Nutrition Info per Serving:
calories: 790 | fat: 60g | protein: 60g | carbs: 2g | net carbs: 1.6g | sugar: 3g | fibre: 0.4g

Crispy Pork Chop with Parmesan

Prep time: 15 minutes | Cook time: 9 to 14 minutes | Serves 4

2 large eggs
50 g finely grated Parmesan cheese
50 g finely ground blanched almond flour
1 tsp. paprika
½ tsp. dried oregano
½ tsp. garlic powder
Salt, Freshly ground black pepper, to taste
600g (2-cm-thick) boneless pork chops
Avocado oil spray

1. Beat the eggs in a shallow bowl. In a separate bowl, combine the Parmesan cheese, almond flour, paprika, oregano, garlic powder, and salt and pepper to taste.
2. Dip the pork chops into the eggs, then coat them with the Parmesan mixture, gently pressing the coating onto the meat. Spray the breaded pork chops with oil.
3. Set the air fryer to 205°C.. Place the pork chops in the air fryer basket in a single layer, working in batches if necessary. Cook for 6 minutes. Flip the chops and spray them with more oil. Cook for another 3 to 8 minutes, until an instant-read thermometer reads 60°C.
4. Allow the pork chops to rest for at least 5 minutes, and then serve.

Nutrition Info per Serving:

calories: 351 | fat: 20g | protein: 38g | carbs: 4g | net carbs: 2g | sugar: 4.4g | fibre: 2g

Beef Chuck with Brussels Sprouts

Prep time: 30 minutes | Cook time: 25 minutes | Serves 4

455 g beef chuck shoulder steak
2 tbsps. olive oil
1 tbsp. red wine vinegar
1 tsp. fine sea salt
½ tsp. ground black pepper
1 tsp. smoked paprika
1 tsp. onion powder
½ tsp. garlic powder
230 g Brussels sprouts, cleaned and halved
½ tsp. fennel seeds
1 tsp. dried basil
1 tsp. dried sage

1. Firstly, marinate the beef with olive oil, wine vinegar, salt, black pepper, paprika, onion powder, and garlic powder. Rub the marinade into the meat and let it stay for at least for 3 hours.
2. Air fry at 200ºC for 10 minutes. Pause the machine and add the prepared Brussels sprouts, sprinkle them with fennel seeds, basil, and sage.
3. Turn the machine to 190ºC press the power button and cook for 5 more minutes. Pause the machine, stir and cook for further 10 minutes.
4. Next, remove the meat from the cooking basket and cook the vegetables a few minutes or more if needed and according to your taste. Serve with your favorite mayo sauce.

Nutrition Info per Serving:

calories: 272 | fat: 14g | protein: 26g | carbs: 6g | net carbs: 3g | sugar: 0g | fibre: 3g

Spicy Chicken Roll-Up with Monterey Jack

Prep time: 10 minutes | Cook time: 14 to 17 minutes | Serves 8

910 g boneless, skinless chicken breasts or thighs
1 tsp. chili powder
½ tsp. smoked paprika
½ tsp. ground cumin
Sea salt
Freshly ground black pepper
170 g Monterey Jack cheese, shredded
115 g canned diced green chilies
Avocado oil spray

1. Place the chicken in a large zip-top bag or between two pieces of plastic wrap. Using a meat mallet or heavy skillet, pound the chicken until it is about ½ cm thick.
2. In a small bowl, combine the chili powder, smoked paprika, cumin, and salt and pepper to taste. Sprinkle both sides of the chicken with the seasonings.
3. Sprinkle the chicken with the Monterey Jack cheese, then the diced green chiles.
4. Roll up each piece of chicken from the long side, tucking in the ends as you go. Secure the roll-up with a toothpick.
5. Set the air fryer to 180ºC. Spray the outside of the chicken with avocado oil. Place the chicken in a single layer in the basket, working in batches if necessary, and cook for 7 minutes. Flip and cook for another 7 to 10 minutes, until an instant-read thermometer reads 70ºC.
6. Remove the chicken from the air fryer and allow it to rest for about 5 minutes before serving.

Nutrition Info per Serving:

calories: 192 | fat: 9g | protein: 28g | carbs: 2g | net carbs: 1g | sugar: 6g | fibre: 1g

Turkey Sausage with Cauliflower

Prep time: 45 minutes | Cook time: 28 minutes | Serves 4

455 g turkey mince
1 tsp. garlic pepper
1 tsp. garlic powder
⅓ tsp. dried oregano
½ tsp. salt
25 g onions, chopped
½ head cauliflower, broken into florets
⅓ tsp. dried basil
½ tsp. dried thyme, chopped

1. In a mixing bowl, thoroughly combine the turkey mince, garlic pepper, garlic powder, oregano, salt, and onion, stir well to combine. Spritz a nonstick skillet with pan spray, form the mixture into 4 sausages.
2. Then, cook the sausage over medium heat until they are no longer pink, for approximately 12 minutes.
3. Arrange the cauliflower florets at the bottom of a baking dish. Sprinkle with thyme and basil, spritz with pan spray. Top with the turkey sausages.
4. Roast for 28 minutes at 190ºC, turning once halfway through. Eat warm.

Nutrition Info per Serving:

calories: 289 | fat: 25g | protein: 11g | carbs: 3g | net carbs: 2g | sugar: 0g | fibre: 1g

Buttery Strip Steak

Prep time: 7 minutes | Cook time: 12 minutes | Serves 6

115 g unsalted butter, at room temperature
100 g finely grated Parmesan cheese
25 g finely ground
blanched almond flour
680 g New York strip steak
Sea salt, freshly ground black pepper, to taste

1. Place the butter, Parmesan cheese, and almond flour in a food processor. Process until smooth. Transfer to a sheet of parchment paper and form into a log. Wrap tightly in plastic wrap. Freeze for 45 minutes or refrigerate for at least 4 hours.
2. While the butter is chilling, season the steak liberally with salt and pepper. Let the steak rest at room temperature for about 45 minutes.
3. Place the grill pan or basket in your air fryer, set it to 205ºC, and let it preheat for 5 minutes.
4. Working in batches, if necessary, place the steak on the grill pan and cook for 4 minutes. Flip and cook for 3 minutes or more, until the steak is brown on both sides.
5. Remove the steak from the air fryer and arrange an equal amount of the Parmesan butter on top of each steak. Return the steak to the air fryer and continue cooking for another 5 minutes, until an instant-read thermometer reads 50ºC for medium-rare and the crust is golden brown (or to your desired doneness).
6. Transfer the cooked steak to a plate, let it rest for 10 minutes before serving.

Nutrition Info per Serving:

calories: 465 | fat: 37g | protein: 33g | carbs: 2g | net carbs: 1g | sugar: 6.1g | fibre: 1g

Courgette Noodle with Beef Meatball

Prep time: 15 minutes | Cook time: 11 to 13 minutes | Serves 6

455 g beef mince
1½ tsps. sea salt, plus more for seasoning
1 large egg, beaten
1 tsp. gelatin
75 g Parmesan cheese
2 tsps. minced garlic
1 tsp. Italian seasoning
Freshly ground black pepper, to taste
Avocado oil spray
Keto-friendly marinara sauce, for serving
170 g Courgette noodles, made using a spiralizer or store-bought

1. Place the beef mince in a large bowl, and season with the salt.
2. Place the egg in a separate bowl and sprinkle with the gelatin. Allow it to sit for 5 minutes.
3. Stir the gelatin mixture, then pour it over the beef mince. Add the Parmesan, garlic, and Italian seasoning. Season with salt and pepper.
4. Form the mixture into 11-cmmeatballs and place them on a plate, cover with plastic wrap and refrigerate for at least 1 hour or overnight.
5. Spray the meatballs with oil. Set the air fryer to 205°C and arrange the meatballs in a single layer in the air fryer basket. Cook for 4 minutes. Flip the meatballs and spray them with more oil. Cook for 4 minutes or more, until an instant-read thermometer reads 71ºC. Transfer the meatballs to a plate and allow them to rest.
6. While the meatballs are resting, heat the marinara in a saucepan on the stove over medium heat.
7. Place the courgette noodles in the air fryer, and cook at 205ºC for 3 to 5 minutes.
8. To serve, place the courgette noodles in serving bowls. Top with meatballs and warm marinara.

Nutrition Info per Serving:

calories: 312 | fat: 25g | protein: 20g | carbs: 2g | net carbs: 1g | sugar: 0g | fibre: 1g

Lime Marinated Lamb Chop, page 30

Chicken Breast with Coriander and Lime, page 35

Crispy Pork Chop with Parmesan, page 32

Lush Spiced Ribeye Steak, page 35

Bacon-Wrapped Cheese Pork, page 36

Aromatic Pork Loin Roast, page 36

34　Chapter 5 Meat and Poultry

Lush Spiced Ribeye Steak

Prep time: 20 minutes | Cook time: 15 minutes | Serves 3

680 g ribeye, bone-in
1 tbsp. butter, room temperature
Salt, to taste
½ tsp. crushed black pepper
½ tsp. dried dill
½ tsp. cayenne pepper
½ tsp. garlic powder
½ tsp. onion powder
1 tsp. ground coriander
3 tbsps. mayonnaise
1 tsp. garlic, minced

1. Start by preheating your Air Fryer to 205ºC.
2. Pat dry the ribeye and rub it with softened butter on all sides. Sprinkle with seasonings and transfer to the cooking basket.
3. Cook in the preheated Air Fryer for 15 minutes, flipping them halfway through the cooking time.
4. In the meantime, simply mix the mayonnaise with garlic and place in the refrigerator until ready to serve. Bon appétit!

Nutrition Info per Serving:
calories: 437 | fat: 24g | protein: 51g | carbs: 2g | net carbs: 1g | sugar: 0g | fibre: 1g

Chicken Breast with Coriander and Lime

Prep time: 10 minutes | Cook time: 15 minutes | Serves 4

For the Chicken:
1 tsp. turmeric
1 diced large onion
1 tbsp. avocado oil
1 tsp. garam masala
1 tsp. smoked paprika
1 tsp. ground fennel seeds
455-g chicken breast, boneless & skinless
2 tsps. minced ginger
2 tsps. minced garlic cloves
nonstick cooking oil spray
salt & cayenne pepper, to taste
To Top:
15 g chopped coriander
2 tsps. juiced lime

1. Make slight piercing all over the chicken breast then set aside.
2. Using a large mixing bowl add in all the remaining ingredients and combine together.
3. Add the pierced chicken breast into the bowl then set aside for an hour to marinate.
4. Transfer the marinated chicken and veggies into the fryer basket then coat with the cooking oil spray.
5. Cook for 15 minutes at 180ºC then serve and enjoy with a garnish of coriander topped with the juiced lime.

Nutrition Info per Serving:
calories: 305 | fat: 23g | protein: 19g | carbs: 6g | net carbs: 5g | sugar: 0g | fibre: 1g

Roasted Chicken Leg with Leeks

Prep time: 20 minutes | Cook time: 18 minutes | Serves 6

2 leeks, sliced
2 large-sized tomatoes, chopped
3 cloves garlic, minced
½ tsp. dried oregano
6 chicken legs, boneless and skinless
½ tsp. smoked cayenne pepper
2 tbsps. olive oil
A freshly ground nutmeg

1. In a mixing dish, thoroughly combine all ingredients, minus the leeks. Place in the refrigerator and let it marinate overnight.
2. Lay the leeks onto the bottom of an Air Fryer cooking basket. Top with the chicken legs.
3. Roast chicken legs at 190ºC for 18 minutes, turning halfway through. Serve with hoisin sauce.

Nutrition Info per Serving:
calories: 390 | fat: 15g | protein: 12g | carbs: 7g | net carbs: 6g | sugar: 2g | fibre: 1g

Loin Steak with Mayo

Prep time: 20 minutes | Cook time: 15 minutes | Serves 4

220 g mayonnaise
1 tbsp. fresh rosemary, finely chopped
2 tbsps. Worcestershire sauce
Sea salt, to taste
½ tsp. ground black pepper
1 tsp. smoked paprika
1 tsp. garlic, minced
680 g short loin steak

1. Combine the mayonnaise, rosemary, Worcestershire sauce, salt, pepper, paprika, and garlic, mix to combine well.
2. Now, brush the mayonnaise mixture over both sides of the steak. Lower the steak onto the grill pan.
3. Grill in the preheated Air Fryer at 200ºC for 8 minutes. Turn the steaks over and grill for an additional 7 minutes.
4. Check for doneness with a meat thermometer. Serve warm and enjoy!

Nutrition Info per Serving:
calories: 620 | fat: 50g | protein: 40g | carbs: 3g | net carbs: 2g | sugar: 1g | fibre: 1g

Chapter 5 Meat and Poultry

Aromatic Pork Loin Roast

Prep time: 55 minutes | Cook time: 55 minutes | Serves 6

680 g boneless pork loin roast, washed
1 tsp. mustard seeds
1 tsp. garlic powder
1 tsp. porcini powder
1 tsp. shallot powder
¾ tsp. sea salt flakes
1 tsp. red pepper flakes, crushed
2 dried sprigs thyme, crushed
2 tbsps. lime juice

1. Firstly, score the meat using a small knife, make sure to not cut too deep.
2. In a small-sized mixing dish, combine all seasonings in the order listed above, mix to combine well.
3. Massage the spice mix into the pork meat to evenly distribute. Drizzle with lemon juice.
4. Then, set your Air Fryer to cook at 180ºC . Place the pork in the Air Fryer basket, roast for 25 to 30 minutes. Pause the machine, check for doneness and cook for 25 minutes or more.

Nutrition Info per Serving:
calories: 278 | fat: 16g | protein: 31g | carbs: 2g | net carbs: 1g | sugar: 0g | fibre: 1g

Bacon-Wrapped Cheese Pork

Prep time: 10 minutes | Cook time: 20 minutes | Serves 4

4 (2-cm thick) boneless pork chops
2 (150 g) packages Boursin cheese
8 slices thin-cut bacon

1. Spray the air fryer basket with avocado oil. Preheat the air fryer to 205°C.
2. Place one of the chops on a cutting board. With a sharp knife held parallel to the cutting board, make a 2cm-wide incision on the top edge of the chop. Carefully cut into the chop to form a large pocket, leaving a 1-cm border along the sides and bottom. Repeat with the other 3 chops.
3. Snip the corner of a large resealable plastic bag to form a 1 ½ cm hole. Place the Boursin cheese in the bag and pipe the cheese into the pockets in the chops, dividing the cheese evenly among them.
4. Wrap 2 slices of bacon around each chop and secure the ends with toothpicks. Place the bacon-wrapped chops in the air fryer basket and cook for 10 minutes, then flip the chops and cook for another 8 to 10 minutes, until the bacon is crisp, the chops are cooked through, and the internal temperature reaches 60°C.
5. Store the leftovers in an airtight container in the refrigerator for up to 3 days. Reheat in a preheated 205°C air fryer for 5 minutes, or until warmed through.

Nutrition Info per Serving:
calories: 608 | fat: 45g | protein: 37g | carbs: 16g | net carbs: 15g | sugar: 10g | fibre: 1g

Pork Meatballs

Prep time: 15 minutes | Cook time: 7 minutes | Serves 3

455 g pork mince
1 tbsp. coconut aminos
1 tsp. garlic, minced

2 tbsps. spring onions, finely chopped
50 g Parmesan cheese, preferably freshly grated

1. Combine the pork mince, coconut aminos, garlic, and spring onions in a mixing dish. Mix until everything is well incorporated.
2. Form the mixture into small meatballs.
3. Roll the meatballs over the Parmesan.
4. Cook at 190ºC for 3 minutes, shake the basket and cook for an additional 4 minutes or until meatballs are browned on all sides. Bon appétit!

Nutrition Info per Serving:
calories: 539 | fat: 43g | protein: 32g | carbs: 3g | net carbs: 2g | sugar: 5.6g | fibre: 1g

Skirt Steak with Rice Vinegar

Prep time: 20 minutes | Cook time: 12 minutes | Serves 5

910 g skirt steak
2 tbsps. keto tomato paste
1 tbsp. olive oil
1 tbsp. coconut aminos
60 ml rice vinegar

1 tbsp. fish sauce
Sea salt, to taste
½ tsp. dried dill
½ tsp. dried rosemary
¼ tsp. black pepper, freshly cracked

1. Place all ingredients in a large ceramic dish, let it marinate for 3 hours in your refrigerator.
2. Coat the sides and bottom of the Air Fryer with cooking spray.
3. Add your steak to the cooking basket, reserve the marinade. Cook the skirt steak in the preheated Air Fryer at 205ºC for 12 minutes, turning over a couple of times, basting with the reserved marinade.
4. Bon appétit!

Nutrition Info per Serving:
calories: 401 | fat: 21g | protein: 51g | carbs: 2g | net carbs: 1g | sugar: 0g | fibre: 1g

Chapter 6 Fish and Seafood

Savory Prawns

Prep time: 5 minutes | Cook time: 8 to 10 minutes | Serves 4

455 g fresh large prawns, peeled and deveined
1 tbsp. avocado oil
2 tsps. minced garlic, divided
½ tsp. red pepper flakes
Sea salt and freshly ground black pepper, to taste
2 tbsps. unsalted butter, melted
2 tbsps. chopped fresh parsley

1. Place the prawns in a large bowl and toss with the avocado oil, 1 tsp. of minced garlic, and red pepper flakes. Season with salt and pepper.
2. Set the air fryer to 180ºC. Arrange the prawns in a single layer in the air fryer basket, working in batches if necessary. Cook for 6 minutes. Flip the prawns and cook for 2 to 4 minutes or more, until the internal temperature of the prawns reaches 50ºC. (The time it takes to cook will depend on the size of the prawn.)
3. While the prawns are cooking, melt the butter in a small saucepan over medium heat and stir in the remaining 1 tsp. of garlic.
4. Transfer the cooked prawns to a large bowl, add the garlic butter, and toss well. Top with the parsley and serve warm.

Nutrition Info per Serving:
calories: 220 | fat: 11g | protein: 28g | carbs: 2g | net carbs: 1g | sugar: 0.7g | fibre: 1g

Swordfish Skewers with Cherry Tomato

Prep time: 10 minutes | Cook time: 6 to 8 minutes | Serves 4

455 g filleted swordfish
60 ml avocado oil
2 tbsps. freshly squeezed lemon juice
1 tbsp. minced fresh parsley
2 tsps. Dijon mustard
Sea salt, freshly ground black pepper, to taste
85 g cherry tomatoes

1. Cut the fish into 1-cm chunks, picking out any remaining bones.
2. In a large bowl, whisk together the oil, lemon juice, parsley, and Dijon mustard. Season to taste with salt and pepper. Add the fish and toss to coat the pieces. Cover and marinate the fish chunks in the refrigerator for 30 minutes.
3. Remove the fish from the marinade. Thread the fish and cherry tomatoes on 4 skewers, alternating as you go.
4. Set the air fryer to 205ºC. Place the skewers in the air fryer basket and cook for 3 minutes. Flip the skewers and cook for 3 to 5 minutes longer, until the fish is cooked through and an instant-read thermometer reads 60ºC.

Nutrition Info per Serving:
calories: 315 | fat: 20g | protein: 29g | carbs: 2g | net carbs: 1g | sugar: 2.3g | fibre: 1g

Prawns with Romaine

Prep time: 10 minutes | Cook time: 4 to 6 minutes | Serves 4

340 g fresh large prawns, peeled and deveined
1 tbsp. plus 1 tsp. freshly squeezed lemon juice, divided
4 tbsps. olive oil or avocado oil, divided
2 garlic cloves, minced, divided
¼ tsp. sea salt, plus additional to season the marinade
¼ tsp. freshly ground black pepper, plus additional to season the marinade
65 g mayonnaise
2 tbsps. freshly grated Parmesan cheese
1 tsp. Dijon mustard
1 tinned anchovy, mashed
340 g romaine hearts, torn

1. Place the prawns in a large bowl. Add 1 tbsp. of lemon juice, 1 tbsp. of olive oil, and 1 minced garlic clove. Season with salt and pepper. Toss well and refrigerate for 15 minutes.
2. While the prawn marinates, make the dressing: In a blender, combine the mayonnaise, Parmesan cheese, Dijon mustard, the remaining 1 tsp. of lemon juice, the anchovy, the remaining minced garlic clove, ¼ tsp. of salt, and ¼ tsp. of pepper. Process until smooth. With the blender running, slowly stream in the remaining 3 tbsps. of oil. Transfer the mixture to a jar, seal and refrigerate until ready to serve.
3. Remove the prawns from its marinade and place it in the air fryer basket in a single layer. Set the air fryer to 205°C and cook for 2 minutes. Flip the prawns and cook for 2 to 4 minutes or more, until the flesh turns opaque.
4. Place the romaine in a large bowl and toss with the desired amount of dressing. Top with the prawns and serve immediately.

Nutrition Info per Serving:
calories: 329 | fat: 30g | protein: 16g | carbs: 4g | net carbs: 2g | sugar: 1.2g | fibre: 2g

Grilled Tuna Cake

Prep time: 10 minutes | Cook time: 8 minutes | Serves 4

2 cans canned tuna fish
2 celery stalks, trimmed and finely chopped
1 egg, whisked
50 g Parmesan cheese, grated
1 tsp. whole-grain mustard
½ tsp. sea salt
¼ tsp. freshly cracked black peppercorns
1 tsp. paprika

1. Mix all of the above ingredients in the order listed above, mix to combine well and shape into four cakes, chill for 50 minutes.
2. Place on an Air Fryer grill pan. Spritz each cake with a non-stick cooking spray, covering all sides.
3. Grill at 180ºC for 5 minutes, then, pause the machine, flip the cakes over and set the timer for another 3 minutes. Serve.

Nutrition Info per Serving:
calories: 241 | fat: 11g | protein: 30g | carbs: 2g | net carbs: 1g | sugar: 4g | fibre: 1g

Tuna Avocado Bites

Prep time: 10 minutes | Cook time: 7 minutes | Makes 12 bites

1 (280-g) can tuna, drained
55 g full-fat mayonnaise
1 stalk celery, chopped
1 medium avocado, peeled, pitted, and mashed
50 g blanched finely ground almond flour, divided
2 tsps. coconut oil

1. In a large bowl, mix tuna, mayonnaise, celery, and mashed avocado. Form the mixture into balls.
2. Roll balls in almond flour and spritz with coconut oil. Place balls into the air fryer basket.
3. Adjust the temperature to 205°C and set the timer for 7 minutes.
4. Gently turn tuna bites after 5 minutes. Serve warm.

Nutrition Info per Serving:
calories: 323 | fat: 25g | protein: 17g | carbs: 6g | net carbs: 2g | sugar: 1.1g | fibre: 4g

Lemony Salmon Steak

Prep time: 20 minutes | Cook time: 12 minutes | Serves 2

2 salmon steaks
Coarse sea salt, to taste
¼ tsp. freshly ground black pepper, or more to taste
1 tbsp. sesame oil
Zest of 1 lemon
1 tbsp. fresh lemon juice
1 tsp. garlic, minced
½ tsp. smoked cayenne pepper
½ tsp. dried dill

1. Preheat your Air Fryer to 190ºC. Pat dry the salmon steaks with a kitchen towel.
2. In a ceramic dish, combine the remaining ingredients until everything is well whisked.
3. Add the salmon steaks to the ceramic dish and let them sit in the refrigerator for 1 hour. Now, place the salmon steaks in the cooking basket. Reserve the marinade.
4. Cook for 12 minutes, flipping halfway through the cooking time.
5. Meanwhile, cook the marinade in a small sauté pan over a moderate flame. Cook until the sauce has thickened.
6. Pour the sauce over the steaks and serve. Bon appétit!

Nutrition Info per Serving:
calories: 476 | fat: 16g | protein: 47g | carbs: 3g | net carbs: 2g | sugar: 0g | fibre: 1g

Whitefish Fillet with Green Bean

Prep time: 1 hour 20 minutes | Cook time: 15 minutes | Serves 4

455 g whitefish fillets, minced
230g green beans, finely chopped
30 g spring onions, chopped
1 chili pepper, seeded and minced
1 tbsp. red curry paste
1 tbsp. fish sauce
2 tbsps. apple cider vinegar
1 tsp. water
Sea salt flakes, to taste
½ tsp. cracked black peppercorns
2 tbsps. butter, at room temperature
½ tsp. lemon

1. Add all ingredients in the order listed above to the mixing dish. Mix to combine well using a spatula or your hands.
2. Form into small cakes and chill for 1 hour. Place a piece of aluminum foil over the cooking basket. Place the cakes on foil.
3. Cook at 200ºC for 10 minutes, pause the machine, flip each fish cake over and air-fry for additional 5 minutes. Mound a cucumber relish onto the plates, add the fish cakes and serve warm.

Nutrition Info per Serving:
calories: 231 | fat: 12g | protein: 23g | carbs: 6g | net carbs: 4g | sugar: 0.8g | fibre: 2g

Tuna Steak

Prep time: 10 minutes | Cook time: 12 minutes | Serves 4

455-g tuna steaks, boneless and cubed
1 tbsp. mustard
1 tbsp. avocado oil
1 tbsp. apple cider vinegar

1. Mix avocado oil with mustard and apple cider vinegar.
2. Then brush tuna steaks with mustard mixture and put in the air fryer basket.
3. Cook the fish at 180ºC for 6 minutes per side.

Nutrition Info per Serving:
calories: 230 | fat: 8g | protein: 34g | carbs: 2g | net carbs: 1g | sugar: 0.2g | fibre: 1g

Sweet Tilapia Fillets

Prep time: 5 minutes | Cook time: 14 minutes | Serves 4

2 tbsps. sweetener
1 tbsp. apple cider vinegar
4 tilapia fillets, boneless
1 tsp. olive oil

1. Mix apple cider vinegar with olive oil and sweetener.
2. Then rub the tilapia fillets with the sweet mixture and put in the air fryer basket in one layer.
3. Cook the fish at 180ºC for 7 minutes per side.

Nutrition Info per Serving:
calories: 101 | fat: 2g | protein: 20g | carbs: 0g | net carbs: 0g | sugar: 0.5g | fibre: 0g

Roast Swordfish Steak

Prep time: 30 minutes | Cook time: 20 minutes | Serves 3

3 peppers
3 swordfish steaks
1 tbsp. butter, melted
2 garlic cloves, minced
Sea salt and freshly
ground black pepper, to taste
½ tsp. cayenne pepper
½ tsp. ginger powder

1. Start by preheating your Air Fryer to 205ºC. Brush the Air Fryer basket lightly with cooking oil.
2. Then, roast the peppers for 5 minutes. Give the peppers a half turn, place them back in the cooking basket and roast for another 5 minutes.
3. Turn them one more time and roast until the skin is charred and soft or 5 more minutes. Peel the peppers and set aside.
4. Then, add the swordfish steaks to the lightly greased cooking basket and cook at 205ºC for 10 minutes.
5. Meanwhile, melt the butter in a small saucepan. Cook the garlic until fragrant and add the salt, pepper, cayenne pepper, and ginger powder. Cook until everything is thoroughly heated.
6. Plate the peeled peppers and the roasted swordfish, spoon the sauce over them and serve warm.

Nutrition Info per Serving:
calories: 460 | fat: 17g | protein: 66g | carbs: 5g | net carbs: 4g | sugar: 0.3g | fibre: 1g

Mackerel with Spinach

Prep time: 15 minutes | Cook time: 20 minutes | Serves 5

455 g mackerel, trimmed
1 pepper, chopped
15 g spinach, chopped
1 tbsp. avocado oil
1 tsp. ground black pepper
1 tsp. keto tomato paste

1. In the mixing bowl, mix pepper with spinach, ground black pepper, and tomato paste.
2. Fill the mackerel with spinach mixture.
3. Then brush the fish with avocado oil and put it in the air fryer.
4. Cook the fish at 185ºC for 20 minutes.

Nutrition Info per Serving:
calories: 252 | fat: 16g | protein: 22g | carbs: 2g | net carbs: 1g | sugar: 0.5g | fibre: 1g

Prawn with Swiss Chard

Prep time: 10 minutes | Cook time: 10 minutes | Serves 4

455-g prawns, peeled and deveined
½ tsp. smoked paprika
20 g Swiss chard, chopped
2 tbsps. apple cider vinegar
1 tbsp. coconut oil
60 g heavy cream

1. Mix prawns with smoked paprika and apple cider vinegar.
2. Put the prawns in the air fryer and add coconut oil.
3. Cook the prawns at 180ºC for 10 minutes.
4. Then mix cooked prawns with remaining ingredients and carefully mix.

Nutrition Info per Serving:
calories: 193 | fat: 8g | protein: 26g | carbs: 2g | net carbs: 1g | sugar: 5.3g | fibre: 1g

Lemony Salmon, page 43

Savory Prawns, page 39

Golden Prawn, page 43

Sweet Tilapia Fillets, page 41

Grilled Tuna Cake, page 40

Tuna Steak, page 41

Chapter 6 Fish and Seafood

Tilapia with Balsamic Vinegar

Prep time: 5 minutes | Cook time: 15 minutes | Serves 4

4 tilapia fillets, boneless | 1 tsp. avocado oil
2 tbsps. balsamic vinegar | 1 tsp. dried basil

1. Sprinkle the tilapia fillets with balsamic vinegar, avocado oil, and dried basil.
2. Then put the fillets in the air fryer basket and cook at 185ºC for 15 minutes.

Nutrition Info per Serving:
calories: 96 | fat: 1g | protein: 21g | carbs: 1g | net carbs: 0g | sugar: 0g | fibre: 1g

Salmon Fritters with Courgette

Prep time: 15 minutes | Cook time: 12 minutes | Serves 4

2 tbsps. almond flour | 1 tsp. avocado oil
1 courgette, grated | ½ tsp. ground black pepper
1 egg, beaten
170 g salmon fillet, diced

1. Mix almond flour with courgette, egg, salmon, and ground black pepper.
2. Then make the fritters from the salmon mixture.
3. Sprinkle the air fryer basket with avocado oil and put the fritters inside.
4. Cook the fritters at 190ºC for 6 minutes per side.

Nutrition Info per Serving:
calories: 103 | fat: 5g | protein: 11g | carbs: 3g | net carbs: 2g | sugar: 0g | fibre: 1g

Lemony Salmon

Prep time: 10 minutes | Cook time: 12 minutes | Serves 2

2 (115 g) salmon fillets, skin removed | ½ tsp. garlic powder
2 tbsps. unsalted butter, melted | 1 medium lemon
 | ½ tsp. dried dill

1. Place each fillet on a 10-cm× 10-cm square of aluminum foil. Drizzle with butter and sprinkle with garlic powder.
2. Zest half of the lemon and sprinkle zest over salmon. Slice other half of the lemon and lay two slices on each piece of salmon. Sprinkle dill over salmon.
3. Gather and fold foil at the top and sides to fully close packets. Place foil packets into the air fryer basket.
4. Adjust the temperature to 205°C and set the timer for 12 minutes.
5. Salmon will be easily flaked and have an internal temperature of at least 60°C when fully cooked. Serve immediately.

Nutrition Info per Serving:
calories: 252 | fat: 16g | protein: 20g | carbs: 2g | net carbs: 1g | sugar: 1g | fibre: 1g

Salmon with Cauliflower

Prep time: 10 minutes | Cook time: 25 minutes | Serves 4

455 g salmon fillet, diced | 1 tbsp. coconut oil, melted
105 g cauliflower, shredded | 1 tsp. ground turmeric
1 tbsp. dried coriander | 60 g coconut cream

1. Mix salmon with cauliflower, dried coriander, ground turmeric, coconut cream, and coconut oil.
2. Transfer the salmon mixture in the air fryer and cook the meal at 180ºC for 25 minutes. Stir the meal every 5 minutes to avoid the burning.

Nutrition Info per Serving:
calories: 222 | fat: 14g | protein: 23g | carbs: 3g | net carbs: 2g | sugar: 5.1g | fibre: 1g

Golden Prawn

Prep time: 20 minutes | Cook time: 7 minutes | Serves 4

2 egg whites | 1 tsp. garlic powder
60 g coconut flour | ½ tsp. dried rosemary
100 g Parmigiano-Reggiano, grated | ½ tsp. sea salt
½ tsp. celery seeds | ½ tsp. ground black pepper
½ tsp. porcini powder | 680g prawns, deveined
½ tsp. onion powder

1. Whisk the egg with coconut flour and Parmigiano-Reggiano. Add in seasonings and mix to combine well.
2. Dip your prawns in the batter. Roll until they are covered on all sides.
3. Cook in the preheated Air Fryer at 200ºC for 5 to 7 minutes or until golden brown. Work in batches. Serve with lemon wedges if desired.

Nutrition Info per Serving:
calories: 300 | fat: 11g | protein: 44g | carbs: 7g | net carbs: 6g | sugar: 0.2g | fibre: 1g

Rosemary Prawn Skewers

Prep time: 10 minutes | Cook time: 5 minutes | Serves 5

1.8-kg prawns, peeled
1 tbsp. dried rosemary
1 tbsp. avocado oil
1 tsp. apple cider vinegar

1. Mix the prawns with dried rosemary, avocado oil, and apple cider vinegar.
2. Then sting the prawns into skewers and put in the air fryer.
3. Cook the prawns at 205ºC for 5 minutes.

Nutrition Info per Serving:

calories: 437 | fat: 6g | protein: 83g | carbs: 6g | net carbs: 5g | sugar: 0g | fibre: 1g

Basil Salmon Fillet

Prep time: 10 minutes | Cook time: 8 minutes | Serves 2

280 g salmon fillet
½ tsp. ground coriander
1 tsp. ground cumin
1 tsp. dried basil
1 tbsp. avocado oil

1. In the shallow bowl, mix ground coriander, ground cumin, and dried basil.
2. Then coat the salmon fillet in the spices and sprinkle with avocado oil.
3. Put the fish in the air fryer basket and cook at 200ºC for 4 minutes per side.

Nutrition Info per Serving:

calories: 201 | fat: 9g | protein: 28g | carbs: 1g | net carbs: 0g | sugar: 0g | fibre: 1g

Snapper with Shallot and Tomato

Prep time: 20 minutes | Cook time: 15 minutes | Serves 2

2 snapper fillets
1 shallot, peeled and sliced
2 garlic cloves, halved
1 pepper, sliced
1 small-sized serrano pepper, sliced
1 tomato, sliced
1 tbsp. olive oil
¼ tsp. freshly ground black pepper
½ tsp. paprika
Sea salt, to taste
2 bay leaves

1. Place two parchment sheets on a working surface. Place the fish in the centre of one side of the parchment paper.
2. Top with the shallot, garlic, peppers, and tomato. Drizzle olive oil over the fish and vegetables. Season with black pepper, paprika, and salt. Add the bay leaves.
3. Fold over the other half of the parchment. Now, fold the paper around the edges tightly and create a half moon shape, sealing the fish inside.
4. Cook in the preheated Air Fryer at 200ºC for 15 minutes. Serve warm.

Nutrition Info per Serving:

calories: 329 | fat: 9g | protein: 47g | carbs: 13g | net carbs: 12g | sugar: 1.5g | fibre: 1g

Chapter 7 Snack and Dessert

Strawberry Pecan Pie

Prep time: 15 minutes | Cook time: 10 minutes | Serves 6

165 g whole shelled pecans
1 tbsp. unsalted butter, softened
240 g heavy whipping cream
12 medium fresh strawberries, hulled
2 tbsps. sour cream

1. Place pecans and butter into a food processor and pulse ten times until a dough forms. Press dough into the bottom of an ungreased 12-cm round nonstick baking dish.
2. Place dish into air fryer basket. Adjust the temperature to 160ºC and set the timer for 10 minutes. Crust will be firm and golden when done. Let it cool 20 minutes.
3. In a large bowl, whisk cream until fluffy and doubled in size, for about 2 minutes.
4. In a separate large bowl, mash strawberries until mostly liquid. Fold strawberries and sour cream into whipped cream.
5. Spoon mixture into cooled crust, cover, and place into refrigerator for at least 30 minutes to set. Serve chilled.

Nutrition Info per Serving:
calories: 340 | fat: 33g | protein: 3g | carbs: 7g | net carbs: 4g | sugar: 15g | fibre: 3g

Chocolate Chips Soufflés

Prep time: 5 minutes | Cook time: 15 minutes | Serves 2

2 large eggs, whites and yolks separated
1 tsp. vanilla extract
60 g low-carb chocolate chips
2 tsps. coconut oil, melted

1. In a medium bowl, beat egg whites until stiff peaks form, for about 2 minutes. Set aside. In a separate medium bowl, whisk egg yolks and vanilla together. Set aside.
2. In a separate medium microwave-safe bowl, place chocolate chips and drizzle with coconut oil. Microwave on high 20 seconds, then stir and continue cooking in 10-second increments until melted, being careful not to overheat chocolate. Let it cool 1 minute.
3. Slowly pour melted chocolate into egg yolks and whisk until smooth. Then, slowly begin adding egg white mixture to chocolate mixture, about ¼ cup at a time, folding in gently.
4. Pour mixture into two 8-cm ramekins greased with cooking spray. Place ramekins into air fryer basket. Adjust the temperature to 205°C and set the timer for 15 minutes. Soufflés will puff up while cooking and deflate a little once cooled. The centre will be set when done. Let it cool 10 minutes, then serve warm.

Nutrition Info per Serving:
calories: 217 | fat: 18g | protein: 8g | carbs: 19g | net carbs: 11g | sugar: 9.3g | fibre: 8g

Chocolate Brownies

Prep time: 40 minutes | Cook time: 35 minutes | Serves 8

140 g unsweetened chocolate, chopped into chunks
2 tbsps. instant espresso powder
1 tbsp. cocoa powder, unsweetened
130 g almond butter
50 g almond flour
15 g sweetener
1 tsp. pure coffee extract
½ tsp. lime peel zest
35 g coconut flour
2 eggs plus 1 egg yolk
½ tsp. baking soda
½ tsp. baking powder
½ tsp. ground cinnamon
⅓ tsp. ancho chili powder
For the Chocolate Mascarpone Frosting:
115 g mascarpone cheese, at room temperature
45 g unsweetened chocolate chips
25 g Sweetener
55 g unsalted butter, at room temperature
1 tsp. vanilla paste
A pinch of fine sea salt

1. First of all, microwave the chocolate and almond butter until completely melted, allow the mixture to cool at room temperature.
2. Then, whisk the eggs, Sweetener, cinnamon, espresso powder, coffee extract, ancho chili powder, and lime zest.
3. Next step, add the vanilla/egg mixture to the chocolate/butter mixture. Stir in the almond flour and coconut flour along with baking soda, baking powder and cocoa powder.
4. Finally, press the batter into a lightly buttered cake pan. Air-fry for 35 minutes at 175ºC.
5. In the meantime, make the frosting. Beat the butter and mascarpone cheese until creamy. Add in the melted chocolate chips and vanilla paste.
6. Gradually, stir in the sweetener and salt, beat until everything's well combined. Lastly, frost the brownies and serve.

Nutrition Info per Serving:
calories: 365 | fat: 33g | protein: 7g | carbs: 10g | net carbs: 5g | sugar: 12g | fibre: 5g

Chapter 7 Snack and Dessert

Whiskey Chocolate Brownies

Prep time: 15 minutes | Cook time: 35 minutes | Serves 10

3 tbsps. whiskey
230 g white chocolate
75 g almond flour
20 g coconut flakes
120 ml coconut oil
2 eggs plus an egg yolk, whisked
15 g sweetener
2 tbsps. cocoa powder, unsweetened
¼ tsp. ground cardamom
1 tsp. pure rum extract

1. Microwave white chocolate and coconut oil until everything's melted, allow the mixture to cool at room temperature.
2. After that, thoroughly whisk the eggs, sweetener, rum extract, cocoa powder and cardamom.
3. Next step, add the rum/egg mixture to the chocolate mixture. Stir in the flour and coconut flakes, mix to combine.
4. Mix cranberries with whiskey and let them soak for 15 minutes. Fold them into the batter. Press the batter into a lightly buttered cake pan.
5. Air-fry for 35 minutes at 170ºC. Allow them to cool slightly on a wire rack before slicing and serving.

Nutrition Info per Serving:
calories: 303 | fat: 28g | protein: 5.5g | carbs: 9.1g | net carbs: 7.2g | sugar: 7.7g | fibre: 5.2g

Calamari Rings

Prep time: 10 minutes | Cook time: 15 minutes | Serves 4

2 large egg yolks
100 g powdered Parmesan cheese
30 g coconut flour
3 tsps. dried oregano leaves
½ tsp. garlic powder
½ tsp. onion powder
455 g calamari, sliced into rings
Fresh oregano leaves, for garnish (optional)
265 g no-sugar-added marinara sauce, for serving (optional)
Lemon slices, for serving (optional)

1. Spray the air fryer basket with avocado oil. Preheat the air fryer to 205°C.
2. In a shallow dish, whisk the egg yolks. In a separate bowl, mix together the Parmesan, coconut flour, and spices.
3. Dip the calamari rings in the egg yolks, tap off any excess egg, then dip them into the cheese mixture and coat well. Use your hands to press the coating onto the calamari if necessary. Spray the coated rings with avocado oil.
4. Place the calamari rings in the air fryer, leaving space between them, and cook for 15 minutes, or until golden brown. Garnish with fresh oregano, if desired, and serve with marinara sauce for dipping and lemon slices, if desired.
5. Best served fresh. Store leftovers in an airtight container in the fridge for up to 5 days. Reheat in a preheated 205°C air fryer for 3 minutes, or until heated through.

Nutrition Info per Serving:
calories: 287 | fat: 13g | protein: 28g | carbs: 11g | net carbs: 8g | sugar: 4.3g | fibre: 3g

Avocado Fries

Prep time: 10 minutes | Cook time: 15 minutes | Serves 6

3 firm, barely ripe avocados, halved, peeled, and pitted
200 g parmesan cheese
2 tsps. fine sea salt
2 tsps. ground black pepper
2 tsps. ground cumin
1 tsp. chili powder
1 tsp. paprika
½ tsp. garlic powder
½ tsp. onion powder
2 large eggs
Salsa, for serving (optional)
Fresh chopped coriander leaves, for garnish (optional)

1. Spray the air fryer basket with avocado oil. Preheat the air fryer to 205°C.
2. Slice the avocados into thick-cut french fry shapes.
3. In a bowl, mix together the parmesan, salt, pepper, and seasonings.
4. In a separate shallow bowl, beat the eggs.
5. Dip the avocado fries into the beaten eggs and shake off any excess, then dip them into the parmesan mixture. Use your hands to press the breading into each fry.
6. Spray the fries with avocado oil and place them in the air fryer basket in a single layer, leaving space between them. If there are too many fries to fit in a single layer, work in batches. Cook in the air fryer for 13 to 15 minutes, until golden brown, flipping after 5 minutes.
7. Serve with salsa, if desired, and garnish with fresh chopped coriander, if desired. Best served fresh.
8. Store leftovers in an airtight container in the fridge for up to 5 days. Reheat in a preheated 205°C air fryer for 3 minutes, or until heated through.

Nutrition Info per Serving:
calories: 282 | fat: 22g | protein: 15g | carbs: 9g | net carbs: 2g | sugar: 0g | fibre: 7g

Spinach Chips

Prep time: 20 minutes | Cook time: 10 minutes | Serves 3

90 g fresh spinach leaves
1 tbsp. extra-virgin olive oil
1 tsp. sea salt
½ tsp. cayenne pepper
1 tsp. garlic powder
Chili Yogurt Dip:
60 g yogurt
2 tbsps. mayonnaise
½ tsp. chili powder

1. Toss the spinach leaves with the olive oil and seasonings.
2. Bake in the preheated Air Fryer at 175ºC for 10 minutes, shaking the cooking basket occasionally.
3. Bake until the edges brown, working in batches.
4. In the meantime, make the sauce by whisking all ingredients in a mixing dish. Serve immediately.

Nutrition Info per Serving:
calories: 128 | fat: 12g | protein: 2g | carbs: 3g | net carbs: 2g | sugar: 6.8g | fibre: 1g

Kale Chips

Prep time: 5 minutes | Cook time: 10 minutes | Makes 8 cups

½ tsp. dried chives
½ tsp. dried dill weed
½ tsp. dried parsley
¼ tsp. garlic powder
¼ tsp. onion powder
⅛ tsp. fine sea salt
⅛ tsp. ground black pepper
2 large bunches kale

1. Spray the air fryer basket with avocado oil. Preheat the air fryer to 180ºC.
2. Place the seasonings, salt, and pepper in a small bowl and mix well.
3. Wash the kale and pat completely dry. Use a sharp knife to carve out the thick inner stems, then spray the leaves with avocado oil and sprinkle them with the seasoning mix.
4. Place the kale leaves in the air fryer in a single layer and cook for 10 minutes, shaking and rotating the chips halfway through. Transfer the baked chips to a baking sheet to cool completely and crisp up. Repeat with the remaining kale. Sprinkle the cooled chips with salt before serving, if desired.
5. Kale chips can be stored in an airtight container at room temperature for up to 1 week, but they are best eaten within 3 days.

Nutrition Info per Serving:
calories: 11 | fat: 1g | protein: 1g | carbs: 2g | net carbs: 1g | sugar: 0g | fibre: 1g

Salami Roll-Ups

Prep time: 5 minutes | Cook time: 4 minutes | Makes 16 roll-ups

115 g cream cheese, broken into 16 equal pieces
16 (15 g) deli slices Genoa salami

1. Place a piece of cream cheese at the edge of a slice of salami and roll to close. Secure with a toothpick. Repeat with remaining cream cheese pieces and salami.
2. Place roll-ups in an ungreased 12-cm round nonstick baking dish and place into air fryer basket. Adjust the temperature to 175°C and set the timer for 4 minutes. Salami will be crispy and cream cheese will be warm when done. Let it cool 5 minutes before serving.

Nutrition Info per Serving:
calories: 269 | fat: 22g | protein: 11g | carbs: 2g | net carbs: 2g | sugar: 5.6g | fibre: 0g

Orange Custard

Prep time: 15 minutes | Cook time: 40 minutes | Serves 6

6 eggs
200 g cream cheese, at room temperature
2½ cans condensed milk, sweetened
10 g sweetener
½ tsp. orange rind, grated
1½ cardamom pods, bruised
2 tsps. vanilla paste
60 ml fresh orange juice

1. In a saucepan, melt sweetener over a moderate flame, it takes about 10 to 12 minutes. Immediately but carefully pour the melted sugar into six ramekins, tilting to coat their bottoms, allow them to cool slightly.
2. In a mixing dish, beat the cheese until smooth, now, fold in the eggs, one at a time, and continue to beat until pale and creamy.
3. Add the orange rind, cardamom, vanilla, orange juice, and the milk, mix again. Pour the mixture over the caramelized sugar. Air-fry, covered, at 160ºC for 28 minutes or until it has thickened.
4. Refrigerate overnight, garnish with berries or other fruits and serve.

Nutrition Info per Serving:
calories: 247 | fat: 18.8g | protein: 10.7g | carbs: 7.8g | net carbs: 6.1g | sugar: 7.4g | fibre: 0g

Kale Chips, page 48

Avocado Fries, page 47

Air Fried Aubergine, page 50

Coconut and Chocolate Pudding, page 52

Bacon-Wrapped Onion Rings, page 50

Chicken Nuggets, page 52

Chapter 7 Snack and Dessert   49

Pepperoni Chips

Prep time: 5 minutes | Cook time: 8 minutes | Serves 2

14 slices pepperoni

1. Place pepperoni slices into ungreased air fryer basket. Adjust the temperature to 175°C and set the timer for 8 minutes. Pepperoni will be browned and crispy when done. Let it cool 5 minutes before serving. Store in airtight container at room temperature up to 3 days.

Nutrition Info per Serving:
calories: 69 | fat: 5g | protein: 3g | carbs: 0g | net carbs: 0g | sugar: 0g | fibre: 0g

Bacon-Wrapped Onion Rings

Prep time: 5 minutes | Cook time: 10 minutes | Serves 8

1 large white onion, peeled and cut into 16 (1/2-cm-thick) slices
8 slices bacon

1. Stack 2 slices onion and wrap with 1 slice bacon. Secure with a toothpick. Repeat with remaining onion slices and bacon.
2. Place onion rings into ungreased air fryer basket. Adjust the temperature to 175°C and set the timer for 10 minutes, turning rings halfway through cooking. Bacon will be crispy when done. Serve warm.

Nutrition Info per Serving:
calories: 84 | fat: 4g | protein: 5g | carbs: 8g | net carbs: 6g | sugar: 3g | fibre: 2g

Coconut Tart with Walnuts

Prep time: 15 minutes | Cook time: 13 minutes | Serves 6

240 ml coconut milk
2 eggs
55 g butter, at room temperature
1 tsp. vanilla essence
¼ tsp. ground cardamom
¼ tsp. ground cloves
40 g walnuts, ground
10 g sweetener
50 g almond flour

1. Begin by preheating your Air Fryer to 180ºC. Spritz the sides and bottom of a baking pan with nonstick cooking spray.
2. Mix all ingredients until well combined. Scrape the batter into the prepared baking pan.
3. Bake approximately 13 minutes, use a toothpick to test for doneness. Bon appétit!

Nutrition Info per Serving:
calories: 230 | fat: 20.4g | protein: 7.1g | carbs: 5g | net carbs: 3.6g | sugar: 6.9g | fibre: 1.5g

Air Fried Aubergine

Prep time: 45 minutes | Cook time: 13 minutes | Serves 4

1 aubergine, peeled and thinly sliced
Salt, to taste
50 g almond flour
60 ml olive oil
120 ml water
1 tsp. garlic powder
½ tsp. dried dill weed
½ tsp. ground black pepper, to taste

1. Salt the aubergine slices and let them stay for about 30 minutes. Squeeze the aubergine slices and rinse them under cold running water.
2. Toss the aubergine slices with the other ingredients. Cook at 200ºC for 13 minutes, working in batches.
3. Serve with a sauce for dipping. Bon appétit!

Nutrition Info per Serving:
calories: 241 | fat: 21g | protein: 4g | carbs: 9g | net carbs: 4g | sugar: 0g | fibre: 5g

Mixed Berry Pots

Prep time: 15 minutes | Cook time: 35 minutes | Serves 6

60 g unsweetened mixed berries
10 g granulated sweetener
2 tbsps. golden flaxseed meal
¼ tsp. ground star anise
½ tsp. ground cinnamon
1 tsp. xanthan gum
65 g almond flour
20 g powdered sweetener
½ tsp. baking powder
25 g unsweetened coconut, finely shredded
55 g butter, cut into small pieces

1. Toss the mixed berries with the granulated sweetener, golden flaxseed meal, star anise, cinnamon, and xanthan gum. Divide between six custard cups coated with cooking spray.
2. In a mixing dish, thoroughly combine the remaining ingredients. Sprinkle over the berry mixture.
3. Bake in the preheated Air Fryer at 165ºC for 35 minutes. Work in batches if needed. Bon appétit!

Nutrition Info per Serving:
calories: 155 | fat: 14.3g | protein: 3.1g | carbs: 5.1g | net carbs: 4g | sugar: 6.8g | fibre: 2.6g

Provolone Cheese Balls

Prep time: 15 minutes | Cook time: 4 minutes | Serves 10

2 eggs, beaten
1 tsp. coconut oil, melted
255 g coconut flour
140 g provolone cheese, shredded
2 tbsps. sweetener
1 tsp. baking powder
¼ tsp. ground coriander
Cooking spray

1. Mix eggs with coconut oil, coconut flour, Provolone cheese, sweetener, baking powder, and ground cinnamon.
2. Make the balls and put them in the air fryer basket.
3. Sprinkle the balls with cooking spray and cook at 205ºC for 4 minutes.

Nutrition Info per Serving:
calories: 176 | fat: 7g | protein: 8g | carbs: 19g | net carbs: 8g | sugar: 4.2g | fibre: 11g

Berry Compote with Coconut Chips

Prep time: 15 minutes | Cook time: 20 minutes | Serves 6

1 tbsp. butter
340 g mixed berries
10 g granulated sweetener
¼ tsp. grated nutmeg
¼ tsp. ground cloves
½ tsp. ground cinnamon
1 tsp. pure vanilla extract
45 g coconut chips

1. Start by preheating your Air Fryer to 165ºC. Grease a baking pan with butter.
2. Place all ingredients, except for the coconut chips, in a baking pan. Bake in the preheated Air Fryer for 20 minutes.
3. Serve in individual bowls, garnished with coconut chips. Bon appétit!

Nutrition Info per Serving:
calories: 176 | fat: 14.3g | protein: 0.6g | carbs: 9.5g | net carbs: 6.8g | sugar: 8.1g | fibre: 2.1g

Courgette Fries

Prep time: 10 minutes | Cook time: 10 minutes | Serves 8

2 medium courgettes, ends removed, quartered lengthwise, and sliced into 6-cm long fries
½ tsp. salt
70 g heavy whipping cream
50 g blanched finely ground almond flour
75 g grated Parmesan cheese
1 tsp. Italian seasoning

1. Sprinkle courgettes with salt and wrap in a kitchen towel to draw out excess moisture. Let it sit 2 hours.
2. Pour cream into a medium bowl. In a separate medium bowl, whisk together flour, Parmesan, and Italian seasoning.
3. Place each courgette fry into cream, then gently shake off excess. Press each fry into dry mixture, coating each side, then place into ungreased air fryer basket. Adjust the temperature to 205°C and set the timer for 10 minutes, turning fries halfway through cooking. Fries will be golden and crispy when done. Place on clean parchment sheet to cool for 5 minutes before serving.

Nutrition Info per Serving:
calories: 124 | fat: 10g | protein: 5g | carbs: 4g | net carbs: 3g | sugar: 6.4g | fibre: 1g

Coconut and Chocolate Pudding

Prep time: 15 minutes | Cook time: 15 minutes | Serves 10

115 g butter
210 g cooking chocolate, unsweetened
1 tsp. liquid stevia

2 tbsps. full fat coconut milk
2 eggs, beaten
25 g coconut, shredded

1. Begin by preheating your Air Fryer to 165ºC.
2. In a microwave-safe bowl, melt the butter, chocolate, and stevia. Allow it to cool to room temperature.
3. Add the remaining ingredients to the chocolate mixture, stir to combine well. Scrape the batter into a lightly greased baking pan.
4. Bake in the preheated Air Fryer for 15 minutes or until a toothpick comes out dry and clean. Enjoy!

Nutrition Info per Serving:
calories: 229 | fat: 21.3g | protein: 4.4g | carbs: 5.4g | net carbs: 4g | sugar: 3.5g | fibre: 3g

Chicken Nuggets

Prep time: 20 minutes | Cook time: 12 minutes | Serves 6

455 g chicken breasts, slice into tenders
½ tsp. cayenne pepper
Salt and black pepper, to taste
25 g almond flour

1 egg, whisked
50 g Parmesan cheese, freshly grated
55 g mayo
60 ml no-sugar-added barbecue sauce

1. Pat the chicken tenders dry with a kitchen towel. Season with the cayenne pepper, salt, and black pepper.
2. Dip the chicken tenders into the almond flour, followed by the egg. Press the chicken tenders into the Parmesan cheese, coating evenly.
3. Place the chicken tenders in the lightly greased Air Fryer basket. Cook at 180ºC or 9 to 12 minutes, turning them over to cook evenly.
4. In a mixing bowl, thoroughly combine the mayonnaise with the barbecue sauce. Serve the chicken nuggets with the sauce for dipping. Bon appétit!

Nutrition Info per Serving:
calories: 268 | fat: 18g | protein: 2g | carbs: 4g | net carbs: 3g | sugar: 3.3g | fibre: 1g

Appendix 1: Measurement Conversion Chart

Volume Equivalents (Dry)

US STANDARD	METRIC (APPROXIMATE)
1/8 teaspoon	0.5 mL
1/4 teaspoon	1 mL
1/2 teaspoon	2 mL
3/4 teaspoon	4 mL
1 teaspoon	5 mL
1 tablespoon	15 mL
1/4 cup	59 mL
1/2 cup	118 mL
3/4 cup	177 mL
1 cup	235 mL
2 cups	475 mL
3 cups	700 mL
4 cups	1 L

Temperatures Equivalents

FAHRENHEIT (F)	CELSIUS(C) (APPROXIMATE)
225 °F	107 °C
250 °F	120 °C
275 °F	135 °C
300 °F	150 °C
325 °F	160 °C
350 °F	180 °C
375 °F	190 °C
400 °F	205 °C
425 °F	220 °C
450 °F	235 °C
475 °F	245 °C
500 °F	260 °C

Volume Equivalents (Liquid)

US STANDARD	US STANDARD (OUNCES)	METRIC (APPROXIMATE)
2 tablespoons	1 fl.oz.	30 mL
1/4 cup	2 fl.oz.	60 mL
1/2 cup	4 fl.oz.	120 mL
1 cup	8 fl.oz.	240 mL
1 1/2 cup	12 fl.oz.	355 mL
2 cups or 1 pint	16 fl.oz.	475 mL
4 cups or 1 quart	32 fl.oz.	1 L
1 gallon	128 fl.oz.	4 L

Weight Equivalents

US STANDARD	METRIC (APPROXIMATE)
1 ounce	28 g
2 ounces	57 g
5 ounces	142 g
10 ounces	284 g
15 ounces	425 g
16 ounces (1 pound)	455 g
1.5 pounds	680 g
2 pounds	907 g

Appendix 2: 365-Day Meal Plan

To use the sheet more efficiently, an alphabetical recipe index is placed at the end of the book. You can find the exact page of the recipe you are looking for quickly.

Day 1-30

DAY-1	DAY-2	DAY-3	DAY-4	DAY-5
Blueberry Muffin	Aubergine Lasagna	Lemony Salmon	Lush Spiced Ribeye Steak	Bacon-Wrapped Onion Rings
DAY-6	**DAY-7**	**DAY-8**	**DAY-9**	**DAY-10**
Chicken Nuggets	Cauliflower with Avocado	Lime Marinated Lamb Chop	Mushroom Soufflés	Rosemary Prawn Skewers
DAY-11	**DAY-12**	**DAY-13**	**DAY-14**	**DAY-15**
Cheese-Broccoli Fritters	Lime Marinated Lamb Chop	Snapper with Shallot and Tomato	Mixed Berry Pots	Lemony Cake
DAY-16	**DAY-17**	**DAY-18**	**DAY-19**	**DAY-20**
Mackerel with Spinach	Riced Cauliflower with Eggs	Provolone Cheese Balls	Golden Biscuits	Ham Chicken with Cheese
DAY-21	**DAY-22**	**DAY-23**	**DAY-24**	**DAY-25**
Buttery Strip Steak	Tuna Steak	Ham Egg	Spinach Chips	Courgette with Spinach
DAY-26	**DAY-27**	**DAY-28**	**DAY-29**	**DAY-30**
Whitefish Fillet with Green Bean	Spinach Omelet	Citrus Courgette Balls	Bacon-Wrapped Cheese Pork	Orange Custard

Day 31-60

DAY-31	DAY-32	DAY-33	DAY-34	DAY-35
Pork Meatballs	Chocolate Chip Muffin	Prawns with Romaine	Cheese Stuffed Pepper	Courgette Fries
DAY-36	**DAY-37**	**DAY-38**	**DAY-39**	**DAY-40**
Cheddar Green Beans	Tuna Avocado Bites	Skirt Steak with Rice Vinegar	Salami Roll-Ups	Ham with Avocado
DAY-41	**DAY-42**	**DAY-43**	**DAY-44**	**DAY-45**
Bacon Lettuce Wraps	Courgette with Spinach	Sweet Tilapia Fillets	Skirt Steak Carne Asada	Strawberry Pecan Pie
DAY-46	**DAY-47**	**DAY-48**	**DAY-49**	**DAY-50**
Basil Salmon Fillet	Beef Chuck with Brussels Sprouts	Sausage with Peppers	Pepperoni Chips	Riced Cauliflower with Eggs

DAY-51	DAY-52	DAY-53	DAY-54	DAY-55
Coconut Tart with Walnuts	Spinach Cheese Casserole	Turkey Sausage with Cauliflower	Spinach and Tomato Egg	Prawn with Swiss Chard
DAY-56	**DAY-57**	**DAY-58**	**DAY-59**	**DAY-60**
Roast Swordfish Steak	Pepperoni Egg	Tofu with Chili-Galirc Sauce	Chocolate Brownies	Roasted Chicken Leg with Leeks

Day 61-90

DAY-61	DAY-62	DAY-63	DAY-64	DAY-65
Chocolate Chips Soufflés	Chicken Breast with Coriander and Lime	Pecan and Almond Granola	Swordfish Skewers with Cherry Tomato	Super Cheese Cauliflower Fritters
DAY-66	**DAY-67**	**DAY-68**	**DAY-69**	**DAY-70**
Salmon Fritters with Courgette	Sausage Egg Cup	Calamari Rings	Aromatic Pork Loin Roast	Cheese-Broccoli Fritters
DAY-71	**DAY-72**	**DAY-73**	**DAY-74**	**DAY-75**
Egg with Cheddar	Coconut and Chocolate Pudding	Beef Chuck with Brussels Sprouts	Roast Aubergine and Courgette Bites	Rosemary Prawn Skewers
DAY-76	**DAY-77**	**DAY-78**	**DAY-79**	**DAY-80**
Aromatic Pork Loin Roast	Cauliflower with Avocado	Prawn with Swiss Chard	Cheese Stuffed Courgette	Kale Chips
DAY-81	**DAY-82**	**DAY-83**	**DAY-84**	**DAY-85**
Citrus Courgette Balls	Snapper with Shallot and Tomato	Courgette Noodle with Beef Meatball	Berry Compote with Coconut Chips	Broccoli and Mushroom Frittata
DAY-86	**DAY-87**	**DAY-88**	**DAY-89**	**DAY-90**
Pork Cutlets with Red Wine	Avocado Fries	Cauliflower Hash Browns	Sweet Tilapia Fillets	Asparagus with Broccoli

Day 91-120

DAY-91	DAY-92	DAY-93	DAY-94	DAY-95
Golden Prawn	Golden Biscuits	Broccoli Croquettes	Pork Tenderloin with Ricotta	Air Fried Aubergine
DAY-96	**DAY-97**	**DAY-98**	**DAY-99**	**DAY-100**
Prawns with Romaine	Super Cheese Cauliflower Fritters	Herbed Lamb Chops with Parmesan	Coconut and Chocolate Pudding	Simple Ham and Pepper Omelet
DAY-101	**DAY-102**	**DAY-103**	**DAY-104**	**DAY-105**

Appendix

Loin Steak with Mayo	Spinach Chips	Lemony Cake	Citrus Courgette Balls	Salmon with Cauliflower
DAY-106	**DAY-107**	**DAY-108**	**DAY-109**	**DAY-110**
Sausage with Peppers	Tilapia with Balsamic Vinegar	Roasted Chicken Leg with Leeks	Aubergine Lasagna	Courgette Fries
DAY-111	**DAY-112**	**DAY-113**	**DAY-114**	**DAY-115**
Cheese Stuffed Pepper	Provolone Cheese Balls	Turkey Sausage with Cauliflower	Spinach Omelet	Whitefish Fillet with Green Bean
DAY-116	**DAY-117**	**DAY-118**	**DAY-119**	**DAY-120**
Mixed Berry Pots	Mushroom Soufflés	Salmon Fritters with Courgette	Skirt Steak with Rice Vinegar	Blueberry Muffin

Day 121-150

DAY-121	**DAY-122**	**DAY-123**	**DAY-124**	**DAY-125**
Tuna Steak	Orange Custard	Cheese-Broccoli Fritters	Ham Chicken with Cheese	Spinach Omelet
DAY-126	**DAY-127**	**DAY-128**	**DAY-129**	**DAY-130**
Coconut Tart with Walnuts	Chocolate Chip Muffin	Sweet Tilapia Fillets	Crispy Pork Chop with Parmesan	Cheese Stuffed Pepper
DAY-131	**DAY-132**	**DAY-133**	**DAY-134**	**DAY-135**
Aromatic Pork Loin Roast	Lemony Salmon	Spinach Cheese Casserole	Berry Compote with Coconut Chips	Ham with Avocado
DAY-136	**DAY-137**	**DAY-138**	**DAY-139**	**DAY-140**
Salami Roll-Ups	Beef Chuck with Brussels Sprouts	Broccoli and Mushroom Frittata	Snapper with Shallot and Tomato	Cheddar Green Beans
DAY-141	**DAY-142**	**DAY-143**	**DAY-144**	**DAY-145**
Pecan and Almond Granola	Swordfish Skewers with Cherry Tomato	Lush Spiced Ribeye Steak	Courgette and Mushroom Kebab	Chicken Nuggets
DAY-146	**DAY-147**	**DAY-148**	**DAY-149**	**DAY-150**
Bacon-Wrapped Cheese Pork	Pepperoni Egg	Whiskey Chocolate Brownies	Broccoli with Herbed Garlic Sauce	Grilled Tuna Cake

Day 151-180

DAY-151	**DAY-152**	**DAY-153**	**DAY-154**	**DAY-155**
Bacon-Wrapped Cheese Pork	Broccoli Frittata	Basil Salmon Fillet	Aubergine with Tomato and Cheese	Provolone Cheese Balls
DAY-156	**DAY-157**	**DAY-158**	**DAY-159**	**DAY-160**

Chicken Nuggets	Lush Spiced Ribeye Steak	Roast Swordfish Steak	Courgette and Mushroom Kebab	Egg with Cheddar
DAY-161	**DAY-162**	**DAY-163**	**DAY-164**	**DAY-165**
Cauliflower Hash Browns	Skirt Steak Carne Asada	Strawberry Pecan Pie	Citrus Courgette Balls	Salmon with Cauliflower
DAY-166	**DAY-167**	**DAY-168**	**DAY-169**	**DAY-170**
Mushroom Soufflés	Chicken Breast with Coriander and Lime	Whitefish Fillet with Green Bean	Ham with Avocado	Coconut Tart with Walnuts
DAY-171	**DAY-172**	**DAY-173**	**DAY-174**	**DAY-175**
Prawns with Romaine	Lime Marinated Lamb Chop	Sausage Egg Cup	Mushroom with Artichoke and Spinach	Pepperoni Chips
DAY-176	**DAY-177**	**DAY-178**	**DAY-179**	**DAY-180**
Air Fried Aubergine	Spinach and Tomato Egg	Ham Chicken with Cheese	Roast Aubergine and Courgette Bites	Tilapia with Balsamic Vinegar

Day 181-210

DAY-181	**DAY-182**	**DAY-183**	**DAY-184**	**DAY-185**
Gold Muffin	Lemony Salmon Steak	Cauliflower with Cheese	Crispy Pork Chop with Parmesan	Coconut and Chocolate Pudding
DAY-186	**DAY-187**	**DAY-188**	**DAY-189**	**DAY-190**
Courgette Noodle with Beef Meatball	Broccoli and Mushroom Frittata	Bacon-Wrapped Onion Rings	Aubergine with Tomato and Cheese	Prawn with Swiss Chard
DAY-191	**DAY-192**	**DAY-193**	**DAY-194**	**DAY-195**
Asparagus with Broccoli	Snapper with Shallot and Tomato	Sausage Egg Cup	Roasted Chicken Leg with Leeks	Provolone Cheese Balls
DAY-196	**DAY-197**	**DAY-198**	**DAY-199**	**DAY-200**
Salmon Fritters with Courgette	Herbed Lamb Chops with Parmesan	Chocolate Chips Soufflés	Sausage with Peppers	Citrus Courgette Balls
DAY-201	**DAY-202**	**DAY-203**	**DAY-204**	**DAY-205**
Courgette Fries	Simple Ham and Pepper Omelet	Riced Cauliflower with Eggs	Spicy Chicken Roll-Up with Monterey Jack	Tilapia with Balsamic Vinegar
DAY-206	**DAY-207**	**DAY-208**	**DAY-209**	**DAY-210**
Loin Steak with Mayo	Mixed Berry Pots	Spinach Cheese Casserole	Rosemary Prawn Skewers	Ham with Avocado

Day 211-240

DAY-211	DAY-212	DAY-213	DAY-214	DAY-215
Salmon Fritters with Courgette	Cheddar Green Beans	Chocolate Chip Muffin	Chocolate Brownies	Ham Chicken with Cheese
DAY-216	**DAY-217**	**DAY-218**	**DAY-219**	**DAY-220**
Spinach Chips	Tofu with Chili-Galirc Sauce	Turkey Sausage with Cauliflower	Whitefish Fillet with Green Bean	Bacon Lettuce Wraps
DAY-221	**DAY-222**	**DAY-223**	**DAY-224**	**DAY-225**
Courgette Noodle with Beef Meatball	Tilapia with Balsamic Vinegar	Cheese-Broccoli Fritters	Ham with Avocado	Orange Custard
DAY-226	**DAY-227**	**DAY-228**	**DAY-229**	**DAY-230**
Roast Swordfish Steak	Courgette and Mushroom Kebab	Simple Ham and Pepper Omelet	Whiskey Chocolate Brownies	Herbed Lamb Chops with Parmesan
DAY-231	**DAY-232**	**DAY-233**	**DAY-234**	**DAY-235**
Cheese Stuffed Courgette	Avocado Fries	Loin Steak with Mayo	Lemony Salmon Steak	Lemony Cake
DAY-236	**DAY-237**	**DAY-238**	**DAY-239**	**DAY-240**
Mackerel with Spinach	Super Cheese Cauliflower Fritters	Pepperoni Chips	Pecan and Almond Granola	Crispy Pork Chop with Parmesan

Day 241-270

DAY-241	DAY-242	DAY-243	DAY-244	DAY-245
Pork Cutlets with Red Wine	Whiskey Chocolate Brownies	Blueberry Muffin	Broccoli with Herbed Garlic Sauce	Mackerel with Spinach
DAY-246	**DAY-247**	**DAY-248**	**DAY-249**	**DAY-250**
Golden Biscuits	Pork Meatballs	Salami Roll-Ups	Spinach Cheese Casserole	Tuna Avocado Bites
DAY-251	**DAY-252**	**DAY-253**	**DAY-254**	**DAY-255**
Cheese-Broccoli Fritters	Ham Egg	Sweet Tilapia Fillets	Crispy Pork Chop with Parmesan	Mixed Berry Pots
DAY-256	**DAY-257**	**DAY-258**	**DAY-259**	**DAY-260**
Rosemary Prawn Skewers	Mushroom with Artichoke and Spinach	Loin Steak with Mayo	Sausage with Peppers	Bacon-Wrapped Onion Rings
DAY-261	**DAY-262**	**DAY-263**	**DAY-264**	**DAY-265**
Skirt Steak Carne Asada	Asparagus with Broccoli	Air Fried Aubergine	Salmon Fritters with Courgette	Spinach Omelet

DAY-266	DAY-267	DAY-268	DAY-269	DAY-270
Mushroom Soufflés	Prawns with Romaine	Coconut Tart with Walnuts	Spinach and Tomato Egg	Roasted Chicken Leg with Leeks

Day 271-300

DAY-271	DAY-272	DAY-273	DAY-274	DAY-275
Cheese Stuffed Courgette	Whitefish Fillet with Green Bean	Courgette Noodle with Beef Meatball	Provolone Cheese Balls	Egg with Cheddar
DAY-276	DAY-277	DAY-278	DAY-279	DAY-280
Spinach and Tomato Egg	Pepperoni Chips	Citrus Courgette Balls	Spicy Chicken Roll-Up with Monterey Jack	Salmon Fritters with Courgette
DAY-281	DAY-282	DAY-283	DAY-284	DAY-285
Aromatic Pork Loin Roast	Cauliflower Hash Browns	Calamari Rings	Roast Swordfish Steak	Spinach Cheese Casserole
DAY-286	DAY-287	DAY-288	DAY-289	DAY-290
Pork Meatballs	Tuna Avocado Bites	Broccoli and Mushroom Frittata	Courgette and Mushroom Kebab	Orange Custard
DAY-291	DAY-292	DAY-293	DAY-294	DAY-295
Chicken Nuggets	Broccoli Frittata	Lemony Salmon Steak	Mushroom with Artichoke and Spinach	Buttery Strip Steak
DAY-296	DAY-297	DAY-298	DAY-299	DAY-300
Chocolate Chips Soufflés	Super Cheese Cauliflower Fritters	Sausage with Peppers	Lime Marinated Lamb Chop	Lemony Salmon

Day 301-330

DAY-301	DAY-302	DAY-303	DAY-304	DAY-305
Grilled Tuna Cake	Cheese Stuffed Courgette	Pork Tenderloin with Ricotta	Courgette Fries	Lemony Cake
DAY-306	DAY-307	DAY-308	DAY-309	DAY-310
Riced Cauliflower with Eggs	Berry Compote with Coconut Chips	Blueberry Muffin	Basil Salmon Fillet	Crispy Pork Chop with Parmesan
DAY-311	DAY-312	DAY-313	DAY-314	DAY-315
Loin Steak with Mayo	Golden Biscuits	Strawberry Pecan Pie	Swordfish Skewers with Cherry Tomato	Tofu with Chili-Galirc Sauce
DAY-316	DAY-317	DAY-318	DAY-319	DAY-320

Spinach Omelet	Buttery Strip Steak	Bacon-Wrapped Onion Rings	Courgette with Spinach	Roast Swordfish Steak
DAY-321	**DAY-322**	**DAY-323**	**DAY-324**	**DAY-325**
Savory Prawns	Cheese-Broccoli Fritters	Ham Egg	Roasted Chicken Leg with Leeks	Spinach Chips
DAY-326	**DAY-327**	**DAY-328**	**DAY-329**	**DAY-330**
Broccoli with Herbed Garlic Sauce	Whiskey Chocolate Brownies	Salmon with Cauliflower	Chocolate Chip Muffin	Turkey Sausage with Cauliflower

Day 331-365

DAY-331	**DAY-332**	**DAY-333**	**DAY-334**	**DAY-335**
Tuna Steak	Ham Chicken with Cheese	Chocolate Chips Soufflés	Pepperoni Egg	Super Cheese Cauliflower Fritters
DAY-336	**DAY-337**	**DAY-338**	**DAY-339**	**DAY-340**
Pecan and Almond Granola	Chicken Breast with Coriander and Lime	Cheese-Broccoli Fritters	Coconut and Chocolate Pudding	Sweet Tilapia Fillets
DAY-341	**DAY-342**	**DAY-343**	**DAY-344**	**DAY-345**
Roast Aubergine and Courgette Bites	Provolone Cheese Balls	Herbed Lamb Chops with Parmesan	Rosemary Prawn Skewers	Spinach and Tomato Egg
DAY-346	**DAY-347**	**DAY-348**	**DAY-349**	**DAY-350**
Salami Roll-Ups	Lemony Cake	Prawns with Romaine	Skirt Steak with Rice Vinegar	Cheese Stuffed Courgette
DAY-351	**DAY-352**	**DAY-353**	**DAY-354**	**DAY-355**
Lush Spiced Ribeye Steak	Chocolate Chip Muffin	Lemony Salmon Steak	Mushroom with Artichoke and Spinach	Whiskey Chocolate Brownies
DAY-356	**DAY-357**	**DAY-358**	**DAY-359**	**DAY-360**
Courgette and Mushroom Kebab	Pepperoni Chips	Pork Tenderloin with Ricotta	Roast Swordfish Steak	Simple Ham and Pepper Omelet
DAY-361	**DAY-362**	**DAY-363**	**DAY-364**	**DAY-365**
Chicken Nuggets	Asparagus with Broccoli	Egg with Cheddar	Pork Cutlets with Red Wine	Salmon with Cauliflower

Appendix 3: Air Fryer Time Table

Beef

Item	Temp (°F)	Time (mins)	Item	Temp (°F)	Time (mins)
Beef Eye Round Roast (4 lbs.)	400 °F	45 to 55	Meatballs (1-inch)	370 °F	7
Burger Patty (4 oz.)	370 °F	16 to 20	Meatballs (3-inch)	380 °F	10
Filet Mignon (8 oz.)	400 °F	18	Ribeye, bone-in (1-inch, 8 oz)	400 °F	10 to 15
Flank Steak (1.5 lbs.)	400 °F	12	Sirloin steaks (1-inch, 12 oz)	400 °F	9 to 14
Flank Steak (2 lbs.)	400 °F	20 to 28			

Chicken

Item	Temp (°F)	Time (mins)	Item	Temp (°F)	Time (mins)
Breasts, bone in (1 ¼ lb.)	370 °F	25	Legs, bone-in (1 ¾ lb.)	380 °F	30
Breasts, boneless (4 oz)	380 °F	12	Thighs, boneless (1 ½ lb.)	380 °F	18 to 20
Drumsticks (2 ½ lb.)	370 °F	20	Wings (2 lb.)	400 °F	12
Game Hen (halved 2 lb.)	390 °F	20	Whole Chicken	360 °F	75
Thighs, bone-in (2 lb.)	380 °F	22	Tenders	360 °F	8 to 10

Pork & Lamb

Item	Temp (°F)	Time (mins)	Item	Temp (°F)	Time (mins)
Bacon (regular)	400 °F	5 to 7	Pork Tenderloin	370 °F	15
Bacon (thick cut)	400 °F	6 to 10	Sausages	380 °F	15
Pork Loin (2 lb.)	360 °F	55	Lamb Loin Chops (1-inch thick)	400 °F	8 to 12
Pork Chops, bone in (1-inch, 6.5 oz)	400 °F	12	Rack of Lamb (1.5 – 2 lb.)	380 °F	22

Fish & Seafood

Item	Temp (°F)	Time (mins)	Item	Temp (°F)	Time (mins)
Calamari (8 oz)	400 °F	4	Tuna Steak	400 °F	7 to 10
Fish Fillet (1-inch, 8 oz)	400 °F	10	Scallops	400 °F	5 to 7
Salmon, fillet (6 oz)	380 °F	12	Shrimp	400 °F	5
Swordfish steak	400 °F	10			

Vegetables

INGREDIENT	AMOUNT	PREPARATION	OIL	TEMP	COOK TIME
Asparagus	2 bunches	Cut in half, trim stems	2 Tbsp	420°F	12-15 mins
Beets	1½ lbs	Peel, cut in ½-inch cubes	1 Tbsp	390°F	28-30 mins
Bell peppers (for roasting)	4 peppers	Cut in quarters, remove seeds	1 Tbsp	400°F	15-20 mins
Broccoli	1 large head	Cut in 1-2-inch florets	1 Tbsp	400°F	15-20 mins
Brussels sprouts	1 lb	Cut in half, remove stems	1 Tbsp	425°F	15-20 mins
Carrots	1 lb	Peel, cut in ¼-inch rounds	1 Tbsp	425°F	10-15 mins
Cauliflower	1 head	Cut in 1-2-inch florets	2 Tbsp	400°F	20-22 mins
Corn on the cob	7 ears	Whole ears, remove husks	1 Tbsp	400°F	14-17 mins
Green beans	1 bag (12 oz)	Trim	1 Tbsp	420°F	18-20 mins
Kale (for chips)	4 oz	Tear into pieces, remove stems	None	325°F	5-8 mins
Mushrooms	16 oz	Rinse, slice thinly	1 Tbsp	390°F	25-30 mins
Potatoes, russet	1½ lbs	Cut in 1-inch wedges	1 Tbsp	390°F	25-30 mins
Potatoes, russet	1 lb	Hand-cut fries, soak 30 mins in cold water, then pat dry	½-3 Tbsp	400°F	25-28 mins
Potatoes, sweet	1 lb	Hand-cut fries, soak 30 mins in cold water, then pat dry	1 Tbsp	400°F	25-28 mins
Zucchini	1 lb	Cut in eighths lengthwise, then cut in half	1 Tbsp	400°F	15-20 mins

Appendix 4: Dirty Dozen and Clean Fifteen

The Environmental Working Group (EWG) is a widely known organization that has an eminent guide to pesticides and produce. More specifically, the group takes in data from tests conducted by the US Department of Agriculture (USDA) and then categorizes produce into a list titled "Dirty Dozen," which ranks the twelve top produce items that contain the most pesticide residues, or alternatively the "Clean Fifteen," which ranks fifteen produce items that are contaminated with the least amount of pesticide residues.

The EWG has recently released their 2021 Dirty Dozen list, and this year strawberries, spinach and kale – with a few other produces which will be revealed shortly – are listed at the top of the list. This year's ranking is similar to the 2020 Dirty Dozen list, with the few differences being that collards and mustard greens have joined kale at number three on the list. Other changes include peaches and cherries, which having been listed subsequently as seventh and eighth on the 2020 list, have now been flipped; the introduction – which the EWG has said is the first time ever – of bell and hot peppers into the 2021 list; and the departure of potatoes from the twelfth spot.

DIRTY DOZEN LIST

- Strawberries
- Spinach
- Kale, collards and mustard greens
- Nectarines
- Apples
- Grapes
- Cherries
- Peaches
- Pears
- Bell and hot peppers
- Celery
- Tomatoes

CLEAN FIFTEEN LIST

- Avocados
- Sweet corn
- Pineapple
- Onions
- Papaya
- Sweet peas (frozen)
- Eggplant
- Asparagus
- Broccoli
- Cabbage
- Kiwi
- Cauliflower
- Mushrooms
- Honeydew melon
- Cantaloupe

These lists are created to help keep the public informed on their potential exposures to pesticides, which then allows for better and healthier food choices to be made.

This is the advice that ASEQ-EHAQ also recommends. Stay clear of the dirty dozen by opting for their organic versions, and always be mindful of what you are eating and how it was grown. Try to eat organic as much as possible – whether it is on the list, or not.

Appendix 5: Recipes Index

A

Asparagus
Asparagus with Broccoli   23

Aubergine
Aubergine Lasagna   22
Aubergine with Tomato and Cheese   24
Roast Aubergine and Courgette Bites   27
Air Fried Aubergine   50

Avocado
Ham with Avocado   14
Avocado Fries   47

B

Bacon
Bacon Lettuce Wraps   14

Beef
Courgette Noodle with Beef Meatball   33

Beef Chuck Shoulder Steak
Beef Chuck with Brussels Sprouts   32

Berry
Mixed Berry Pots 50
Berry Compote with Coconut Chips   51

Blueberry
Blueberry Muffin 14

Broccoli
Broccoli and Mushroom Frittata   14
Broccoli Frittata   18
Cheese-Broccoli Fritters   22
Broccoli Croquettes   24
Broccoli with Herbed Garlic Sauce   28

C

Calamari
Calamari Rings   47

Cauliflower
Cauliflower with Avocado 16
Cauliflower Hash Browns   18
Super Cheese Cauliflower Fritters   22
Spinach Cheese Casserole   24
Cauliflower with Cheese   26
Riced Cauliflower with Eggs   26

Chicken
Ham Chicken with Cheese   30

Chicken Breast
Spicy Chicken Roll-Up with Monterey Jack   32
Chicken Breast with Coriander and Lime   35
Chicken Nuggets 52

Chicken Leg
Roasted Chicken Leg with Leeks   35

Chocolate
Chocolate Brownies   46
Coconut and Chocolate Pudding   52

Chocolate Chip
Chocolate Chip Muffin   19
Chocolate Chips Soufflés   46

Courgette
Courgette and Mushroom Kebab   23
Courgette with Spinach   26
Citrus Courgette Balls   27
Cheese Stuffed Courgette 28
Salmon Fritters with Courgette   43
Courgette Fries   51

Cremini Mushroom
Mushroom Soufflés   26

G

Green Bean
Cheddar Green Beans   23

Green Pepper
Ham Egg   19

H

Ham
Simple Ham and Pepper Omelet   15

K

Kale

64   Appendix

Kale Chips   48

L
Lamb Chop
Lime Marinated Lamb Chop   30
Herbed Lamb Chops with Parmesan   31

M
Mackerel
Mackerel with Spinach   41

N
New York Strip Steak
Buttery Strip Steak   33

P
Pecan
Pecan and Almond Granola   16
Pepper
Cheese Stuffed Pepper   24
Pepperoni
Pepperoni Egg   20
Pepperoni Chips 50
Pork
Pork Meatballs   37
Pork Chop
Crispy Pork Chop with Parmesan   32
Bacon-Wrapped Cheese Pork   36
Pork Cutlet
Pork Cutlets with Red Wine   31
Pork Loin Roast
Aromatic Pork Loin Roast 36
Pork Sausage
Sausage Egg Cup 15
Sausage with Peppers   18
Pork Tenderloin
Pork Tenderloin with Ricotta   31
Portobello Mushroom
Mushroom with Artichoke and Spinach   27
Prawn

Savory Prawns   39
Prawns with Romaine   39
Prawn with Swiss Chard   41
Golden Prawn   43
Rosemary Prawn Skewers 44
Ribeye Steak
Lush Spiced Ribeye Steak 35
Roma Tomato
Spinach and Tomato Egg   20

S
Salami
Salami Roll-Ups   48
Salmon
Lemony Salmon Steak   40
Lemony Salmon   43
Salmon with Cauliflower   43
Basil Salmon Fillet   44
Short Loin Steak
Loin Steak with Mayo   35
Skirt Steak
Skirt Steak Carne Asada   30
Skirt Steak with Rice Vinegar   37
Snapper
Snapper with Shallot and Tomato 44
Spinach
Spinach Omelet 19
Spinach Chips   48
Strawberry
Strawberry Pecan Pie   46
Swordfish
Swordfish Skewers with Cherry Tomato   39
Roast Swordfish Steak   41

T
Tilapia
Sweet Tilapia Fillets   41
Tilapia with Balsamic Vinegar   43
Tofu
Tofu with Chili-Galirc Sauce   23
Tuna
Grilled Tuna Cake   40

Tuna Avocado Bites   40
Tuna Steak   41

Turkey
Turkey Sausage with Cauliflower   33

W

Walnut
Coconut Tart with Walnuts   50

White Chocolate
Whiskey Chocolate Brownies   47

White Onion
Bacon-Wrapped Onion Rings   50

Whitefish
Whitefish Fillet with Green Bean   40

Dear Readers,

We are glad that you purchased this book, your opinion is very important to us. If you have any comments and suggestions on this cookbook, we sincerely invite you to send us an email for feedback.

With your participation, we will grow faster and better.

After receiving your email, we will upgrade the product according to your needs and give you an e-book of 50 recipes as a gift.

We are committed to continuous growth and progress, providing readers with cookbooks that help create a better kitchen life and a healthy body.

I wish you happy every day.

Company contact email: Healthrecipegroup@outlook.com

Printed in Great Britain
by Amazon